The Seaman
Book II

The Seaman

Book II
S. E. ELLACOTT

Abelard-Schuman

London   New York   Toronto

LONDON	NEW YORK	TORONTO
Abelard-Schuman	Abelard-Schuman	Abelard-Schuman
Limited	Limited	Canada Limited
8 King Street	257 Park Avenue South	228 Yorkland Boulevard
WC2	NY 10010	425

Contents

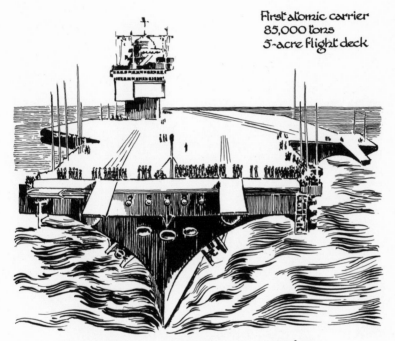

First atomic carrier
85,000 tons
5-acre flight deck

U.S. AIRCRAFT-CARRIER 'ENTERPRISE', 1961.

Author's Preface

This book is intended as a companion work to my history of the soldier in the ranks, *Spearman to Minuteman* and *Conscripts on the March*. Though *The Seaman* is chiefly concerned with ratings, it is not possible to treat them as a separate unit in the same way as the soldier. There is such an interdependence between seamen, officers, and ship that all three have to be considered together. Nevertheless, this work does not present a complete history of ships, but simply examples of progress as affecting the seaman.

S. E. Ellacott

Braunton, North Devon
September, 1969.

A*

1
Skilled in Seafaring

While the American struggle was going on, an epic of southern exploration unfolded under the direction of a British farm laborer's son. James Cook (1728–1779), apprentice storekeeper, collier foremast hand, collier mate, was born at Marton, near Guisborough, in the North Riding of Yorkshire. He volunteered for the Navy in 1755, to avoid the press, and served in H.M.S. *Eagle*. In spite of his father's lowly position, Cook had been educated at the village school, where he displayed remarkable keenness in mathematics. This served him so well as an able seaman that Captain Palliser of *Eagle*, impressed with Cook's ability, used his influence to have him appointed Master in H.M.S. *Mercury*, 24.

While cruising in the St. Lawrence estuary, and along nearby coasts, Cook did such valuable work in sounding and charting those waters that he was chosen to lead a scientific expedition on behalf of the Royal Society. This was intended to observe, from the central southern Pacific, the passage of Venus across the sun, in the spring of 1759. To head the undertaking, Cook was commissioned as lieutenant—an unheard-of rise for a former able seaman. He chose for his voyage the shallow-draft bark *Endeavour*, 370 tons, which was closely packed with men. In addition to 20 officers and 67 crew, there were four artists, Henry Green, an astronomer from Greenwich Observatory, Joseph Banks, a wealthy botanist, and Lars Solander, a Swedish naturalist.

Conditions on the voyage were unique. There had never

11

been a commander who attended so carefully to the welfare of the ship's company. Two main precautions were strictly observed—one against scurvy, the other to banish dirt. Numerous antiscurvy preparations already existed. *Sauerkraut*, a German preparation, consisted of shredded greens in vinegar. Thickened lemon juice, molasses, and malt were used as well, and *portable soup*—thick stew dried and cut into cubes for storing. It was reconstituted in boiling water.

CAPTAIN COOK.

Cook arranged to have all these items combined in a *wort* or medical preparation, which was regularly included in everyone's diet. He carried out frequent personal inspection of the crew's condition, and no chance of obtaining green food was neglected—for instance, a shore party gathered wild celery in Tierra del Fuego.

In the matter of cleanliness the commander was equally careful. He enforced a routine of cold baths. Sanitation was strictly supervised, and the whole ship was constantly under cleaning operations. At the same time, Cook paid great attention to dry quarters; stoves were kept going below, even in the midday heat, to keep the deck dry. As a result of his care, on the whole voyage, there were only three slight scurvy cases, easily cured.

Though the crew tended to regard the regime as rather fussy, the clean bill of health gained their respect, and a great spirit of contentment reigned aboard. For this reason, the rigors of Cape Horn were cheerfully endured. Cook chose that route rather than the Straits of Magellan, despite the prospect of a buffeting. *Endeavour*'s shallow build was a disadvantage in wild water, but this was balanced by her useful tacking qualities. Cook's extensive charting of the region was of immense value to seamen who followed him into those waters. By mid-April he had reached the South Sea Islands, and the transit of Venus was duly observed from a base in Tahiti (June 4, 1769). Southward he ran then, to navigate the coastal regions of New Zealand for 2,400 miles of accurate charting, while the scientific team filled their notebooks.

One of the most creditable features of that expedition was Cook's longitude fixes by means of lunar calculations. Harrison's Chronometer had been ready at the time of sailing, but Cook was not issued with one. A Nautical Almanac, the first, had been published in 1767 by Dr. Nevil Maskelyne, the Astronomer Royal, but it only contained tables of declination and distance estimates for the moon and fixed stars. With the help of the commander's mathematical skill, Henry Green the astronomer assembled invaluable longitude readings.

From the New Zealand coast Cook passed over to Australia, to anchor in the haven they called Botany Bay through Mr. Banks's rapture at the flora there. After leaving the anchorage in May, 1770, Cook named the next great bay

13

Port Jackson, after the Secretary to the Admiralty, but he missed the present Sydney haven.

There followed an extraordinary 1,000-mile voyage between the coast and the Great Barrier Reef, unknown until then. Though soundings were constantly taken, they ran aground once, on the reef called *Endeavour*. More than fifty tons of weight were jettisoned, chiefly guns and ballast.

When she finally came free, there was some underwater damage. That was competently dealt with by Midshipman Monkhouse, who had once seen the operation of *fothering* a leak at sea. Handfuls of mixed wool and oakum (rope fiber) were sewn thickly over a studding sail, and a skilful swimmer dived under the ship to carry a line from the sail to the opposite gunwale. While seamen hauled in the line under control, the swimmer guided the fothered sail below the surface until the inrush of water drew in the sail to plug the leak.

This could only be a temporary repair, so the ship was careened in the mouth of the Endeavour River, where a monument now marks the spot. Here the kangaroo was seen by Europeans for the first time; Mr. Banks found out its name by contact with aborigines. Finally, the explorers' vessel passed into the open sea 150 miles to the northward, by a difficult passage that Cook named Providential Channel. In mid-October 1770, the voyagers reached Batavia, in the East Indies, where they stayed for two months. This fatal place undid much of Cook's great work for his ship's company. Scores of them sickened with fever and dysentery, officers, crew, and passengers alike, so that when *Endeavour* reached home in June, 1771, her people numbered 54 instead of 94. For many years after that epic voyage, the bark worked as a collier in the North Sea.

Though space will not permit a detailed coverage of Cook's succeeding ventures, it is worthy of remark that he chose for them two Whitby colliers, *Resolution*, 462 tons, and *Advent-*

ure, 336 tons. Cook was promoted to commander on his second commission, which was to find more information on Australia, and penetrate the Arctic region. Only four men were lost, one of them through sickness. Such low mortality for those times was undoubtedly due to the commander's care, as before. He saw to it that the seamen changed wet clothes, and that their persons and hammock rolls were clean as well as dry. This cleanliness also applied to the ships, and to galley utensils.

After his second voyage (July, 1772 to July, 1775) Cook was made Post-Captain. He was by far the most famous navigator in the world at that time, and the authorities despatched him on a third expedition in July, 1776. This time he was directed to seek a northeast passage around the North American coast. With the same two ships, he reached the northern extremity late in the season. Conditions were so bitter that he returned to winter in the Sandwich Islands.

Cook's destiny had drawn him to those distant regions. His ships reached Hawaii in mid-January, 1779, and after a false start, he had to return in mid-February to repair storm damage. There was trouble with the islanders; they attacked a water party, and stole a cutter. With a squad of marines Cook went ashore to seize the king by subterfuge. A scuffle developed. Cook shot a man, and was himself stabbed and dragged into the crowd of natives. Later they gave up a few remains of the great seaman, and these were buried at sea, with full military honors. History had strangely repeated itself—Magellan, then Cook, each eminent in his own time, each losing his life in an obscure struggle for a trifling cause.

On board Cook's ship, there always existed the highest mutual regard between the seamen and their commander, but his kindly humanity was certainly not widespread throughout the Royal Navy. As Cook was a man of the people, an able seaman raised to become captain, it is possible that *rapport* was established more easily. In the Navy as a whole there was

15

a great deal of discontent. Over 42,000 seamen deserted during the six years 1774–1780, and at the end of the American War, in 1783, many crews were riotous over delays in paying off. An active mutiny in *Raisonnable*, 64, was

A ROYAL NAVY SEAMAN, 1777.

quelled by the captain, who went forward armed, and persuaded the crew to surrender the ringleaders.

In H.M.S. *Invincible*, 74, at Portsmouth (April, 1780), the crew refused to weigh for the West Indies until they had their six months' pay. This action incurred the death penalty under the Articles of War. *Alexander*, 74, was brought alongside without deterring the obstinate-seamen. At last the

16

authorities gave in, though two of the leaders were punished with 500 lashes.

Among seamen, there is no more notorious name than that of William Bligh (1754–1817), captain of the armed transport *Bounty* in December, 1787. He had been one of Cook's officers on the second Australian voyage, and in 1787 he was commissioned for the South Seas on a curious quest. It was to convey breadfruit plants to the West Indies, as a source of food for plantation slaves. Two gardeners were included among the 44 men of *Bounty*'s company, while

THE 'BOUNTY' MUTINY.

Bligh was both captain and purser—a harsh, violent bully, totally unfit for command. As purser he swindled the men by laying in a short stock of cheap provisions, to keep part of the purchase grant for himself, and he threatened to flog any man who complained. On the pretence that a cheese had been stolen, he stopped such rations of cheese as would balance the loss.

When the ship anchored in Tahiti (October, 1788), the captain's severity redoubled. He cut down the rum issue, and took over all the officers' supplies, saying that he would have

17

nine-tenths of every man's property. A midshipman who slept on watch, during which time three men deserted, was kept in irons for nearly three months. However, while the breadfruit plants were being put on board, the crew were able to enjoy the pleasures of that beautiful island, though Bligh treated the natives harshly. After taking on a supply of coconuts for issue, *Bounty* headed for the Tonga group on April 4, 1789.

During the ensuing three weeks, matters went from bad to worse. Between the crew's reluctance to leave Tahiti, and Bligh's bitter treatment of them, a tense situation arose. In such a case, the captain's position was firmly defined; naval discipline placed the crew completely in his power. Whatever atrocities he committed, behind him were the Articles of War, the irons, the cat and the rope.

The climax came when Bligh publicly accused Acting-Lieutenant Fletcher Christian of stealing coconuts, and cursed him and the other officers. Christian determined at first to swim ashore at Tonga, but he then changed to the idea of taking over the ship. Four men who had recently been flogged helped Christian to distribute weapons, and the captain was seized in his cabin. He and 18 others, officers and men, were put into the ship's cutter, with food, spirits, navigating instruments and charts. For their defense, four cutlasses were passed into the little craft, which was so low in the water that three or four seamen who wished to leave the ship could not be taken. This left Christian with 28 others, including officers and three midshipmen, aboard *Bounty*, which was immediately put about for Tahiti.

On reaching the island, the midshipmen and 13 others wished to stay there, so Christian and the rest set out to seek some more remote place. They found this in Pitcairn's Island, which had been called after its discoverer in 1767; it was one of the most southerly of the scattered South Pacific islands. Here, with native wives, the mutineers formed a settlement,

in company with a group of Tahitian men. Though the
community was reduced by murders and disease, families
grew up and intermarried, so that the present-day islanders
number well over a hundred.

Captain Bligh and his castaway crew, left alone on a waste
of water, lost no time in setting a course; their limited
supplies would not brook delay. In spite of his defects as a
commander, Bligh was a highly skilled navigator, and his iron
will maintained at least an adequate ration for much of the
time. Privation began to take its toll at last, and it was
difficult to create a stir among the crew when Bligh was able
to announce, in a scarcely audible voice, that his objective
was in sight. He wrote of the occasion:

"It is not possible for me to describe the pleasure which
the blessing of the sight of this land diffused among us. It
appeared scarce credible to ourselves, than in an open boat,
and so poorly provided, we should have been able to reach
the coast of Timor [an island just south of present-day
Indonesia] in forty-one days after leaving Tofoa; having in
that time run, by our log, a distance of 3,618 miles: and that,
notwithstanding our extreme distress, no one should have
perished on the voyage!"

As soon as Bligh reached home with his report, the frigate
Pandora, 24, with Captain Edward Edwards, was sent to find
the mutineers. *Pandora* arrived off Tahiti late in March, 1791.

In the meantime, two of the seamen on the island had been
murdered over women, and Midshipman Young had died.
Heywood and Stewart, the other midshipmen, gave themselves up. All 12 seamen were confined together on *Pandora*.

Edwards was a merciless man. He had on deck a kind of
box, 11 feet long, with two nine-inch gratings for ventilation.
In this place the fourteen prisoners remained, handcuffed,
with both legs in irons, and subjected to every discomfort
that the vindictive captain could devise. Half-suffocated in
the heat of that wooden coffin, streaming with sweat, the

19

mutineers lay covered with their own filth, and tortured by vermin. Their food was hardly worthy of the name, and the tiny water supply only kept them thirsty

When *Pandora* was passing through Torres Strait, death was at hand, for she struck a reef and foundered. Edwards would not release the mutineers, but the master-at-arms

SHIP'S CAULKER and PURSER, 1788.

dropped in to them the keys of their leg irons. A gallant boatswain's mate, William Moulter, risked his own life as the ship was going down, and pried open the top scuttle of the foul box. Through that opening, ten of the prisoners escaped, still handcuffed, but the others, unable to get clear in time, drowned like trapped rats.

20

After being held by the captain on a small island, without clothes or shelter, scorched by day and frozen by night, the surviving mutineers were transported to the Cape in Dutch vessels. They were tried, on reaching home in August, 1792, and six of the ten were condemned. Bligh and Edwards subsequently reached flag rank as admirals, though evidence at the trial gave rise to the expressed opinion that Bligh was the worst type of commanding officer.

Mutiny was in the air. For centuries, British seamen had been slaves of the whistle and the lash, with the Articles of War looming over all, but the upheaval of the French Revolution (1789) had made seamen receptive to its spirit. Apart from difficulties with men in the service, the Royal Navy was woefully short of crews at the outbreak of the Anglo-French War in 1793. England's intervention in European affairs was caused by the French invasion of the Rhineland and surrounding areas, in the winter of 1792–93. This was a threat to the balance of power in Europe, a major British concern, and it implied difficulties, at least, for Britain's mercantile trade overseas.

It was a strange naval position on either side. France had seamen and ships, but her officer class had been the banished aristocracy, and naval units were ill-handled, under inexpert direction. In the Royal Navy ships and the officer class were there, but not enough men. One form of bait was an increase in the official bounty for volunteers, with competition between great centers. By 1795, several seaports were offering a bounty of £30. Despite such lures, the number of seamen remained low, even after many foreigners, especially Americans, had been enlisted, and felons had received a standing offer to avoid jail by joining the Navy. In March of the same year, an Act was passed whereby each county had to raise a set quota of men—for instance, Yorkshire was called upon for 1,081 men.

A further Act in the following month clamped an embargo

21

upon British shipping until each port had provided a quota, such as the London figure of 5,704 men. Although the fleet was manned, conditions of service were still unsatisfactory for the lower deck, especially as regards pay. An able seaman received 24s. a month—the same rate as in the mid-seventeenth century, though ships' officers of all ranks were receiving pay and half-pay concessions during 1795–96. Various Acts of 1795 permitted the men to allocate part of their pay to their families every month—able seamen at 5d. a day, ordinary seamen at 4d., and Marines at 3d.

There had been a serious outbreak of mutiny in 1794, when the crew of H.M.S. *Culloden*, under Captain Thomas Troubridge, refused to weigh anchor. After a court-martial, five of the eight ringleaders were hanged. This appeared to repress positive action, until February, 1797, when petitions, from practically all the ships of the line at Portsmouth, were received by the Admiralty.

Pay was the chief complaint—slops and necessities were 30 per cent dearer than they had been a century before, yet pay was at the earlier level. Provisions were short in weight and of poor standard, while no vegetables were supplied in port. Sick seamen were not nursed properly, and comforts intended for them were often taken by the attendants. When seamen were off duty through wounds, their pay was stopped pending recovery or discharge as unfit. There was not enough shore liberty in port. Men coming in on one ship might be transferred to another due to sail, so that they neither set foot on shore nor drew their pay.

No reply was forthcoming, so a concerted resistance to orders was planned between crews. Everyone refused to weigh anchor on April 15, 1797. Unpopular officers were put ashore, while nooses were slung from the yards. A commission of three Admirals met the mutineers' delegates, two from each ship, and agreed to practically all their demands. An Act of Parliament proclaimed pardon for the mutineers, but did not specify any feature of their activities, so the ships remained at anchor. Watches were set as normal, but the Marines on each ship were made prisoners, and all guns were loaded.

On May 14, Lord Howe arrived from London with full powers to act for the Admiralty. He brought details of an Act that redressed the men's grievances, so this and his personal popularity put an end to the Portsmouth mutiny. On the 16th, the fleet put to sea under Admiral Duncan, and destroyed the Dutch squadrons drawn up at Camperdown. However, an outbreak occurred among the ships stationed at the Nore, a sandbank at Thames mouth. Here the leader was Richard Parker of Exeter. This was his third tour of duty, for he had been on strength twice before as a midshipman. He was demoted for misbehavior in 1793, and discharged as insane in 1794.

As president of the seamen delegates, Parker presented to the station commander, Vice-Admiral Sir Charles Buckner, a statement of concessions required. These included the demands of the Portsmouth fleet, with others such as the permanent exclusion of officers who had been turned off their ships by the mutineers. As before, the Admiralty promised pardon if the men returned to duty, but Parker refused any conditional offer.

An amazing situation developed by May 31. Parker had hoisted a red flag over his headquarters in H.M.S. *Sandwich*, and practically all the warships in the area were under his command. Three were drawn across the river, so that no vessel could pass without an order signed by Parker. Some tradeships with food cargoes were plundered at this barrier. One of the most remarkable aspects of the affair was that the seamen stayed with their leader. They must have known that there was little to hope for, and certain punishment. In keeping with the fantastic situation, a loyal salute was fired by all ships on the King's birthday, June 4.

23

At that date, the mutineers' fleet comprised 12 ships of the line, two second-rates, six frigates, and six small craft. Meanwhile, the authorities had been taking measures. Two Acts were passed forbidding contact with mutinous units, and citing penalties for sedition, while active preparations went forward. Gun emplacements were set up on each river bank, with red-hot shot in readiness; the buoys had been removed, and ships were ordered down river to attack. All negotiations by the mutineers were rejected, and it was obvious to them that a crisis was at hand. It came as a breakup. *Repulse*, *Leopard*, and *Ardent* left the fleet, sustaining many casualties under the other mutineers' fire. At the same time, furious struggles were raging aboard some remaining ships over the question of leaving.

At last, on June 13, it was generally acknowledged that the mutineers would submit in return for a pardon. This was not forthcoming. Parker and 31 of his subordinates were arrested, and Parker was hanged a week after his trial on June 22. A number of other seamen were hanged, and several were flogged around the fleet. Those imprisoned went either to the Marshalsea prison or to *Eagle*, which at that date was a prison ship lying in the Medway.

Though the 1797 mutinies were the most serious, they were not the last outbreaks of that period. Wholesale hanging and flogging went on in reprisal until the last large-scale mutiny, on *Téméraire*, flagship of Rear-Admiral Duncan, in December, 1801. A feature of that troubled time was the conspicuous loyalty and steadiness of the Marines. This was due to the type of man recruited, for there was no question of taking in low characters. It would have been dangerous to arm such men; therefore, Marines were not easily recruited.

2
Nelson's Navy

During the heyday of Elizabethan seamen, Sir Francis Drake had been the star, even though there were other skilful and daring seamen in his day. Drake's great asset was his faculty for gaining the regard of the ordinary man, whether on the lower deck or in Plymouth streets. A similar gift was possessed by Horatio Nelson (1759–1805), the seamen's idol of the Napoleonic Wars. In spite of the difference in background, type, and outlook—Drake the chunky, forthright seadog, and Nelson the pale, thin clergyman's son—the spark burned in both to call forth the devotion of those who served them.

Nelson's quiet upbringing in the parsonage at Burnham Thorpe, in Norfolk, was no indication of the adventurous seafaring life that was to be his. Navy regulations laid down that an entrant intending to be a midshipman had to serve aboard for two years first, and the minimum age was 13 (11 for an officer's son). Despite this, Horatio Nelson, no officer's son, entered the Royal Navy at 12, in 1771. Similarly, none could be rated as able seaman unless he had served three years at sea, but many ships' books showed men signing on as such. A candidate for lieutenant was required to be 20 years old, and to have served six years at sea, two years as midshipman or master's mate.

As there was no compulsory registration of birth, it was easy to obtain a falsely dated document. Often young boys were on a ship's books for years without being on board, while the captain drew pay for them as sea boys or servants. When going to the examination for lieutenant it was usual to take a forged baptism certificate. Admiral Sir George Elliot, going up to be examined in 1800, when he was a midshipman, bought a baptism certificate filled out by the hall porter, for 5s. It showed him to be 21; he was in fact 16. Evidently this polite fiction was quite well known to the

HORATIO NELSON.

examining officers, for as Sir George and his companions guilelessly brought in their certificates, a member of the board remarked drily that the ink had not dried in 21 years.

These jugglings were immensely valuable for the steps of later promotion. Nelson was captain of *Agamemnon*, 64, in his early thirties, at the time when he first began to make his name resound through the Royal Navy. His activities in the

Mediterranean fleet, which brought him notice, gave him the first of his two permanent injuries. At the siege of Calvi, in Corsica (1794), a round shot struck near him, driving some fragments into the right eye and destroying its sight. This did not impair his remarkable dash in fighting his ship and drawing its crew with him. One famous exploit in those waters was *Agamemnon's* conquest of the great French *Ca Ira*, 80, in March, 1795. Nelson wrote that the latter was "absolutely large enough to take *Agamemnon* in her hold."

While commanding *Captain*, his second ship of the line, Nelson took an outstanding part in the sharp action against the Spanish fleet near Cape St. Vincent (February, 1797). Under Admiral John Jervis, the British force of 15 ships bore up to cut the line of the Spaniards, who totalled 27 sail. There was a brief, close engagement, during which *Captain* was so severely battered that she lost her foretopmast, every rag of canvas, the shrouds and her wheel. This rendered the ship unmanageable, so Nelson had her laid alongside *San Nicolas*, 74. He, the Commodore, sprang aboard her with seamen and a detachment of Marines. Hooked on to the vessel's quarter was the first-rate *San Josef*, 112, from which musketry was directed on the boarders when they had taken the 74. Nelson organized covering fire by the Marines, and scrambled aboard *San Josef* with his seamen to receive surrender. Success in these undertakings had been greatly aided by heavy fire from *Prince George* before the boarders went in.

That was a typical Nelson episode—headlong into battle, yet with well-directed efforts to spare his crew. Only seven men were killed in the 15-minute engagement that took the two Spaniards, while the whole action lost for *Captain* 24 of her crew—a remarkably light casualty list. Nelson had disregarded the Admiral's orders by taking independent action, but it had been so effective that instead of censure, he was created a Knight of the Bath and promoted to

27

Rear-Admiral. Jervis was raised to the peerage as the Earl of St. Vincent.

Barely five months later, in action at Santa Cruz de Teneriffe, in the Canary Islands, Nelson suffered the second of his wounds on service. A bullet in his right elbow made amputation necessary, so the famous empty sleeve and the eye-patch became twin recognition marks.

These engagements were only preliminaries to glory. In May 1798, Bonaparte's Army of the East was heading for Egypt with a fleet of 13 battleships, intending to take over all British holdings in the Middle East. Throughout the Mediterranean summer, Rear-Admiral Sir Horatio Nelson was seeking the French fleet, with orders for its complete destruction. When the search narrowed to eastern waters, Nelson, leading in *Vanguard* his force of 13 battleships, came down finally on a course for Alexandria.

The Frenchmen had anchored in Aboukir Bay, with a line of shoals between them and the land. They were engaged in a manner that displayed the perfection of tactical skill. When the British vessels were anchored in position, half of them were in the shoals to landward of the opponent, while the other half lay to seaward. An example of completely matter-of-fact judgment was recorded by Captain Miller in the log of *Theseus*:

"I observed their shot sweep just over us, and knowing well that at such a moment Frenchmen would not have coolness enough to change their elevation, I closed them suddenly, and running under the arch of their shot, reserved my fire, every gun being loaded with two and some with three round shot, until I had the *Guerrier*'s masts in line and her jib-boom about six feet clear of our rigging; we then opened with such effect that a second breath could not be drawn before her main and mizzen mast were also gone."

Though the French crews defended their ships with the greatest bravery, the pincers of the master seaman had them fast. Much of the heart was taken out of the French when Admiral Bruey's great flagship *L'Orient* blew up with a blaze that lit up the very masthead colors of the contending ships. This was a classic naval action, the attackers sliding into place like machines on each side of the French, and the whole issue decided by gunfire. A most unusual aspect was that all the ships of two fleets were engaged. Most sea battles were fought out by a nucleus of each force, while the remainder only got in odd shots or did no firing at all. Two battleships and two frigates escaped from that sea grave of the French fleet, and the two large units were destroyed later.

When the news of that epic of fighting seamanship spread abroad, the western world realized that in Nelson the British had the supreme leader. He became Lord Nelson of the Nile, and at the same time a national hero, a by-word among seamen and civilians. Nelson's name was made, and though his reputation for leadership and skill was more than maintained, it was for Aboukir that he was remembered.

When the frail Anglo-French peace broke down in 1803, Spain declared war against Britain. There followed Napoleon's intensified urge for the invasion of hated England, and his elaborate global schemes for rendezvous in the West Indies. By this means his Toulon fleet could draw off the Royal Navy in pursuit, while the French warships doubled eastward to meet the Spanish, master the Channel, and invade. All went awry; the allied fleets were hunted into port by tireless British greyhounds, and the Commander-in-Chief, Admiral Villeneuve, lay fuming in Cadiz, stung by Napoleon's intention to replace him.

At length, like a maddened bull at the charge, the French commander led out his 33 ships to seek battle. Over the horizon lay the 27 ships of the Royal Navy, with Lord Nelson commanding in *Victory*, 104. He stood in toward the land in two-column formation when the repeating frigates passed on the message from the blockading ships off Cadiz.

It was October 21, 1805—a fine, slightly hazy day, with a great westerly swell. Nelson was quietly confident in his fleet and himself, knowing that he bore the regard of every seaman around. Such devotion, at his bidding, would make them work ships and guns like fiends. Only the night before, when the dispatch vessel was bearing away with the mailbags, the

Drawn from the author's painting.
H.M.S. 'VICTORY' TODAY.

Admiral learned that a coxswain of *Victory*, in preparing the bags, had forgotten to put in his letter to his wife. At once Nelson gave orders to signal the mailship's return for that letter, saying that the coxswain might fall in the impending battle—his letter must go.

Into the hazy morning slid the long striped hulls, the port lids black against the yellow gun-deck lines. This was known as the Nelson chequer, for it was the Admiral's scheme. Lofty towers of canvas, gilded in the diffused sunlight, appeared like clusters in some enchanted forest, for the light airs precluded a rigid order. Across the heaving swell mounted the strains of martial music; every battleship had its band on deck. This was the last of the great ceremonial seafights, the gentlemanly approach as to a duel. In *Victory* the Admiral, his coat sewn with replicas of his decorations, paced the quarterdeck with his officers in brilliant array. Above them Nelson's message to the Fleet was expressed in flags:

"England expects that every man will do his duty."

Originally the second word has been "confides," but the signal midshipman had suggested the change, as that word had to be spelled out, while "expects" was in the signal book. Now on every ship the thunderous rumble of the gun trucks, as the black muzzles peered beneath the hooked-up port lids. Nelson might well have said of his men, like Henry V:

"I see you stand like greyhounds in the slips,
Straining upon the start."

That tumultuous six-hour battle, off the shoals of Cape Trafalgar, was opened when Villeneuve's flagship *Bucentaure* dropped a 32-pounder ball close to *Victory* at one and a quarter miles. In closing, *Victory* ran the gauntlet of her enemy's fire, giving little in return, until she broke through the French line shortly after midday. In crossing *Bucentaure*'s stern at ten yards range, she raked the French flagship from end to end as each section of double-shotted guns bore in turn. It was for this reason that *Victory*'s fire was reserved—the first carefully-loaded shots were not to be thrown away at long range. Twenty of the opponent's guns were dismounted by that recurring tempest of fire, and *Bucentaure* lost 400 men beneath it.

Victory herself had lost her mizzentopmast, all her studding booms, and her wheel, while still a quarter of a mile short of the line. *Royal Sovereign* was first to pierce it, and

31

Victory, with forty men at her tiller ropes, passed the stricken flagship. Nearby French ships were pounding her with intensive fire as she was drawn up to *Redoubtable*. Nelson was walking the quarter-deck beside his Flag-Captain, Hardy, who suddenly found the Admiral at his feet.

"I trust that your Lordship is not severely wounded."

From the author's painting.

MAIN GUN DECK, H.M.S. VICTORY.
showing Trafalgar 32 pdrs: rolled hammocks: mess table.

"They have done for me at last, Hardy; my backbone is shot through."

Redoubtable's mizzentop was only about fifteen yards away, with soldiers in it; in fact, a few minutes after Nelson's fall, at 1.25 p.m., grenades and musketry inflicted severe casualties along *Victory*'s upper deck. Even as the wounded

Admiral was being taken below, his signal midshipman, John Pollard, opened fire from the afterpart of the poop. Pollard, a skilled musket shot, had observed soldiers crouching in *Redoubtable*'s tops, so with cartridges placed nearby for Marines he knocked out each soldier who rose breast high to fire. Shortly after this episode, *Temeraire* ran aboard

Drawn from the author's painting.

H.M.S. 'VICTORY' : THE COCKPIT.

Redoubtable, bringing about surrender.

Words are feeble aid in expressing the grief and consternation aboard *Victory* as her smitten commander fought for life in the gloomy cockpit. He lay there, confused and shaken by the thunder and vibration of the guns above, and calling continuously for drinks. When Nelson had fully recovered his senses, he urged Hardy to anchor and keep the fleet together.

33

It was clear that with 20 ships lost already, the Franco-Spanish force could not prevail.

Just over three hours after being hit, the Admiral died, and Sir Cuthbert Collingwood took command of the situation. Widespread damage and destruction had been inflicted on each force, and few of the numerous prizes reached port. Next morning, such a gale arose that the battered ships of both fleets were in sore straits, so many masts and spars had been lost, so many shots between wind and water. Ten of the prizes ran ashore on the Spanish coast alone; *Redoubtable* sank while in tow, and the first-rate *Santissima Trinidad* was scuttled. After a deadly struggle, the fleet with its four remaining prizes gained the shelter of Gibraltar. Twenty-seven of the 33 Franco-Spanish battleships had been taken or destroyed—a crushing blow. Never again during the war did French warships appear as a fleet—it was to be blockade-running from thenceforward. Shattered, too, was Napoleon's fondest dream, the invasion of England. He had gathered a huge flotilla of flat-bottomed vessels during the summer of 1805—1,339 armed transports, with 954 unarmed, to carry across the Channel 163,645 men and 9,059 horses. On August 3, two trial embarkations had shown that the whole force could be afloat in 90 minutes. This had been the purpose of the West Indies feint before Trafalgar, to draw off the British forces.

All hope was destroyed by the cataclysm of October 21. Shortly after that, Nelson's body lay preserved in spirits, while the schooner *Pickle* was bearing home the good and the sad news.

Despite the overwhelming sense of loss that pervaded the Royal Navy--even Nelson's detractors were bound to admit his invaluable *rapport* with the seamen—it would have been difficult for him had he survived the war. Neither his standard of education nor his tastes were suitable for peace-time society. He was largely self-taught, and his
34

feminine attachments were unfortunate. After 11 years of marriage to the frigid Frances Herbert, he struck up an alliance with Emma, the attractive but common wife of Sir William Hamilton in 1798–99. Lady Hamilton bore Nelson a daughter, whom they burdened with the name Horatia (1801–1881). However, his will did not include Emma, and the title passed to his brother, the Revd. William Nelson, who died in 1835. Lady Hamilton soon frittered away her estate after her husband's death, and she herself died in poor circumstances at the age of 50 (1815). Horatia married a clergyman, and there were numerous descendants.

Lord Nelson has a unique monument. His body was laid in St. Paul's Cathedral early in January, 1806, after an impressive waterborne procession headed by a State barge, and a lying-in-state. Though he lies in London, his monument is at Portsmouth—his last command, H.M.S. *Victory*, is still preserved there. After 1815, she was placed in reserve, until 1824 when she became the flagship of Portsmouth Command. Until 1922 *Victory* was moored at the great Naval base, but it became obvious that she would suffer serious damage if she remained afloat, so the ship was brought into the Royal Dockyard, and established in No. 2 Dock, the oldest graving dock in the world. By means of public appeal, £120,000 was raised as a restoration fund, and the work of repair was completed in 1928.

Victory is so placed in the Dockyard that the visitor approaching from the main gates sees only her topmasts, by reason of intervening buildings. On rounding the latter, the full beauty of the ship bursts into view.

In the summer of 1966, the author was permitted, for the purpose of study, unrestricted access to *Victory*, through the kindness of the captain at that time, Lieutenant-Commander "Dick" Whittington. These pictures of the ship are drawn from paintings made by the author aboard and around her.

Trafalgar Day on *Victory* with the famous signal flying, is especially impressive. On that day, in the cockpit, with its inscribed spot "Here Nelson died," the deck is strewn with laurel wreaths from every warship in port, the largest being from the Commander-in-Chief, Portsmouth. Nelson's name is vividly alive in the great Naval base, and at the Trafalgar Day officers' dinner glowing tribute is paid to it.

On board *Victory*, every effort has been made to preserve the fabric, and the atmosphere of a ship of the line, though naturally much repair and replacement has been done. During the 1939 war, most of her guns were taken for scrap and replaced by plastic replicas, but the 32-pounders in the picture were actually used at Trafalgar. Fourteen men comprised a gun crew for the 32-pounder, to serve at port or starboard as required. These men slung their hammocks from the deckhead, between the guns, with an allowance of 14 to 20 inches of space per man. As the spaces in each gun bay were allocated alternately to port and starboard watches, who were never there together, the situation was not as crowded as it might seem.

Meals were taken at a "table" formed by a wide board swinging from the deckhead by a rope at each corner. One such table hung in each gun bay. There were eight men to a mess, as in earlier days, and each in turn acted as "cook." He fetched food from the galley, and drew the daily issue of *grog*. This was rum and water, in ratio one to three parts, with sweetened lemon acid. It was called after Admiral Vernon (1684–1757), who first suggested the change from neat rum to the economy issue with water. As the Admiral favored coats of material called *grosgrain* (pronounced *grograin*), he was known as Old Grog, and the watered rum received the same name.

After the meal, each cook cleaned the utensils, used by the mess, including the wooden kids. His duties brought him an extra issue of grog, with which he could entertain a friend, or pay small debts.

36

These were features of everyday organization, but when the ship was cleared for action, with each man at his station, the whole was a great co-operative system. On the gun decks, each crew had a first and second captain, so that the crew could be divided under command should the guns on both sides be in action at once. A mate or a midshipman was responsible for six guns paired in this way (a division), except on the lower deck, where a division comprised four paired 32-pounders. General supervision on each gun deck was carried out by two lieutenants, while the greater part of the crew served the guns. There were 150 men engaged on the main deck 18-pounders, 180 on the middle deck 24-pounders, and 225 on the lower deck. In the magazine, the gunner had 23 helpers, and the purser with 42 men handed powder.

Other crew members were disposed above decks—20 on the forecastle and 55 on the quarterdeck, where stood the captain and the first lieutenant. Seven seamen were distributed through the tops. On the poop were stationed a party of twelve Royal Marines—so entitled on the recommendation of the Earl of St. Vincent—and 108 more were disposed in small groups throughout the upper deck. In that way there was no obstruction where the guns were being fought.

These various combatant units were served by the signals party on the quarterdeck, the surgeon, his mates, and the chaplain in the cockpit, and the storeroom party of four men.

Throughout the ship itself, various routine preparations had been carried out. In the cabins aft, removable bulkheads and canvas screens had been stowed below, to give clear way for the aftermost guns. Below, in the galley, the fire had been put out, and the cook was in the lantern room that lighted the magazine, on duty with the master-at-arms and a rating. On a wooden ship, fire was an ever-present possibility. A fire party, comprising men with noncombatant duties, such as the storeroom party, were drilled to break out the leather hoses and work the washdeck pumps when called for duty.

There were ominous preparations in the cockpit, where the loblolly men (orderlies) laid out the medicine chests, with bandages, and made ready sails whereon the wounded lay, to be dressed in rotation. This work was done in the dim light of battle lanterns, and the appalling difficulties of surgery under such conditions can hardly be imagined. Gangrene was the terror; an amputation might appear to be successful, then the fatal symptoms showed, bringing horrible death.

3
Britons and Americans at War

A most valuable record of everyday life on a ship of the line, in the Trafalgar period, was made by a seaman of *Revenge*, who served in the battle. He entitled his chronicle *Nautical Economy*,* and produced it under the pseudonym of Jack Nastyface.

Jack was a volunteer, so he took interested note of his new surroundings. For instance, he wrote a careful account of the watch system, and the daily routine. Each watch, starboard and larboard in turn, had four hours' duty and four hours' rest, except for the period between 4 p.m. and 8 p.m., which was divided into two dog watches of two hours each. By this means the duties worked out evenly every 48 hours. There was a further division of time into half-hours, each represented by one stroke on the ship's bell, and timed with a sandglass. Eight bells signified the end of a four-hour watch.

During the first watch, 8 p.m. to midnight, the officer of the watch had the log hove, to check the ship's speed, and this was entered in the ship's logbook, with any other observations. At eight bells the boatswain's mate on duty called the watch below (the off-duty seamen) to work the ship in the "middle watch" (12 midnight to 4 a.m.). They became for that time the watch on deck. Some of the members "holystoned" the deck with "hand bibles"—they knelt upon the wetted deck, scrubbing it with fine gravel under blocks of stone. It was this devotional attitude that called forth the irreverent names. By eight bells the deck was

* Published by Wm. Robins, 9, Staining Lane, London, c. 1836.

swabbed and dried, and the boatswain's mate piped all hands to breakfast. This could be *burgoo* (coarse oatmeal and water) or *Scotch coffee*, burned bread boiled in water with sugar.

After breakfast, the larboard watch began its spell at one bell in the forenoon watch (8.30 a.m.). Their duties consisted of working the ship and holystoning, with the help of iron scrapers, while the ship's cooks were preparing the dinner. When six bells struck (11 a.m.) all hands were called to witness punishment—men who had given offense, knowingly or otherwise, were whipped by the boatswain's mates, each with a cat-o'-nine-tails.

Jack witnessed a flogging around the fleet. For this the offender was put into a launch, with his wrists lashed to a capstan bar rigged fore and aft. It had a stocking over it so that the bound man should not tear off flesh in his agony. Boatswain's mates did the flogging, each delivering six strokes in turn, as they had been trained to do when practicing on a barrel. They were watched very closely to see that they were doing their duty, and that they cleared the lashes after every stroke by drawing them through their fingers. Twenty-five strokes might be delivered at each ship, and after four or five ships the offender's back "resembles so much putrefied liver, and every stroke of the cat brings away the congealed blood." If the seaman was sinking under the lash, wine was poured down his throat, and the doctor, feeling his pulse, might order his removal to the sick bay. When he had recovered there, the sentence was completed—perhaps 500 lashes in all.

This was a court-martial matter, but a ship's captain could order up to five dozen lashes at will, without formality. A petty thief was more severely punished by "running the gauntlet"—he was actually dragged, in a tub with a seat, around the deck, while his shipmates lashed him in turn—a total of several hundred strokes.

Formal punishments like those did not count the practice of "starting" the men while on their duties. Each petty officer might carry a knotted rope's end—the "starter"—and if he chose, he could have off the seaman's outer garments before beating him. Jack noted that sometimes the coat could not be worn for days at a time, through excessive starting. Prime seamen, expert at a topman's duties, might be beaten if they were not thought quick enough, which caused the men to take undue risks. Often such seamen deserted, forsaking pay and prize money dues; *Revenge* was manned three times over in seven years. Her complement consisted of over 600 men, but 2,100 had been on the ship's books during that time.

Those books were subject to much juggling and falsification throughout the Royal Navy. In July 1800, Lieutenant William Walker, of the gunboat *Sparkler*, was court-martialled at Portsmouth for a list of offenses. He had often continued to draw pay for a deserter, and he always drew for 50 men, far in excess of his actual crew. Worse effrontery was the entry of his son, aged one, upon the books; he actually sent a seaman ashore to draw the £5 bounty by pretending to be young Walker.

Recruitment for the Navy still relied much upon the press, and during the Trafalgar period the Government issued a general warrant authorizing widespread seizure for service. A further development was the Impress Service, which provided a large number of press warrants without dates. By this means a pool of potential or actual seamen could be gathered in special Admiralty tenders, for issue to ships as required.

These tenders were absolute pigsties, into which the pressed men were crammed under the vilest conditions. Filthy and clean, well-clothed and ragged, seasick and sound, all were bundled below, and the gratings were clapped over them. More than one seaman wrote of the appalling smells of excreta, body odor, and vomit that blew up revoltingly from

41

the hold of the tender. It is extraordinary that the "receiving ships," on which volunteers were gathered, appeared to offer the same conditions. Those men who boarded the receiver clean were soon as lousy as any beggar, and they were battened below like convicts, while Marine guards with fixed bayonets stood above them. However, if there was a

U.S. NAVY DRESS, 1812-1820.

complaint of foul air below, the officer of the watch was permitted to bring the volunteers on deck.

This was the seamy side of Navy life, but it was forgotten for a time when the liberty men descended on the Point at Portsmouth. For shoregoing, the seaman wore his dark blue kersey jacket, with anchor buttons of metal. It was taped with white to reinforce the seams at the back, and along the sleeves. His trousers and waistcoat might be white, striped with red or blue, and the shirt style varied through plain colors, stripes, or checks. Seamen from the West Indies station wore straw hats in a chosen style, but the general wear was a round type in leather, or canvas japanned. One accessory that tends to mislead was the black neckerchief—a number of historians interpreted this as a sign of mourning for Nelson. In fact, it was introduced at the beginning of the pigtail era, about 1785, to keep the tar on the pigtail away from the coat. Seamen wore that hairstyle until after the Napoleonic wars; the last instance on record was seen aboard H.M.S. *Ganges* in 1823.

During the first decade of the nineteenth century, there was a good deal of friction between America and the warring nations of Europe. Its beginnings as regards Britain arose in the autumn of 1798, when Captain Loring in H.M.S. *Carnatic* stopped and searched an American warship for British deserters. An official Congress directive was issued to all U.S. ships in December, 1798, requiring them to resist as long as possible in such cases. If forced to strike, they should give up the ship with the men, but never the men without the ship. As the *Carnatic* incident was the first recorded, President John Adams told Congress that British conduct had been exemplary before, and that no doubt the slip would be corrected.

At that time there was much great provocation from France. Under an embargo on all vessels trading with Britain, the French had taken and plundered about thirty American tradeships during 1797, and the Directory had refused compensation. Congress pushed ahead with the completion of six frigates that had been laid down in 1794. They were not built up any further at the time because, to the sensitive American public, a peacetime navy could represent a threat to liberty. These beautiful American vessels had almost fishlike lines, with the keel of 150 feet and the mainmast standing 180 feet above deck. *United States*, 44, was the first to be completed, in May, 1797, and she was rapidly followed by *Constellation*, 38, *Constitution*, 44, *President*, 44, and *Chesapeake*, 38. Each frigate carried 30 24-pounders on the gun deck.

In view of the superior conditions in American warships, it is not surprising that a number of British deserters took service aboard. President Adams refused to employ the press; instead he made the service attractive. A basic monthly rate of $15.00 to $17.00 for the able seaman was up to $7.00 more than the rate in a tradeship. Prize money was offered at a fixed rate per ton and per gun, with doubled value if the prize was bigger than her captor. Prospective recruits were invited to inspect crews' quarters, and sample the food. It was claimed that a seaman in the U.S. Navy had more to eat in two days than a Royal Navy rating had in a week. There was certainly a generous issue—6 pounds of meat per man per week, with 1 pound of salt fish, ½ pound of cheese, ¼ pound of butter, 2 pounds of potatoes, a pint of rice, 1½ pints of peas, 6 ounces of molasses, 7 pounds of bread, and half a gallon of spirits or a gallon of beer.

There was another great difference, in the approach to gunnery. Constant practice was maintained by the Americans, while the Admiralty begrudged ammunition expenditure of that kind. Ratings in the U.S. Navy named the individual guns, and created a competitive interest in sea gunnery. In addition to continual gun drill, there was practice in firing blank and target shooting, whereas in the Royal Navy there was no established drill—all depended on the captain's views.

Constellation carried out the Americans' first war operation in early February, 1799. She fought the French frigate *Insurgente*, 44. This vessel was reputed to be the fastest in the world, but *Constellation* overtook her and forced surrender in an hour. Thomas Truxtun, the victor's wealthy captain, followed this by battering almost to pieces the

French *Vengeance*, 52; though almost dismasted, she got away in the darkness.

Encounters like this cut the teeth of the young American Navy. When peace was made with the French in 1800, the small nucleus of 13 frigates that was maintained provided squadrons for Mediterranean duty, beginning in 1801. On this service, Stephen Decatur made his name as a fearless leader. He was with the force of six vessels commanded by Edward Prebble, a sour martinet in the late forties. Prebble's officers were all ten or fifteen years younger than he—in fact, he described them as a "pack of boys." Despite his stiff manner, the commander gained respect by his boldness. He overawed the Sultan of Tangier, by a show of force with double-shotted guns, so that the latter renewed his trading treaties.

Decatur's chance came when *Philadelphia*, 38, was sent into Tripoli but cast away on an uncharted reef, so that gunboats from the shore took the ship. It was the season of winter storms, so Prebble laid down a close blockade of the town, cutting down the corn traffic to nothing. Early in February, 1804, Decatur took in a captured ketch, renamed *Intrepid*, on a kind of cutting-out expedition directed at *Philadelphia*. He could not bring her out, in the usual way, as the Moors had sent down her yards. Still, with his 84 cutlass-armed seamen he proposed to burn the ship.

Though Decatur came in sight of his objective on February 7, a storm prevented his entry into the anchorage before Tripoli until eight days later. He had with him Salvator Catalano, a Sicilian pilot, whose quick wit and knowledge of the language bluffed the guards. No operation could have been neater. In a matter of minutes, on getting aboard, the ship was in Decatur's hands, and his well-drilled crew had set the combustibles. Like the bursting out of a volcano, *Philadelphia* sent the brilliant columns of flame into the dark sky, lighting up the fleet *Intrepid* as she skimmed among the plunging shot from the shore batteries. Not a man was lost, and Decatur was promoted to Captain, with a gold presentation sword, while the pilot received American citizenship.

During the summer, Prebble was building up a force to deliver a telling attack upon Tripoli. He borrowed a number of Neapolitan gunboats and mortar boats, to balance the defenders' five ships and 19 gunboats. On August 3 Decatur and Lieutenant Richard Somers led in the American gunboat flotilla, followed by the frigates. When the latter drew under the castle walls, their tempest of gunfire drove the Moors from their pieces. Decatur was in a fighting fury. He took one large ship by boarding, as well as a gunboat in which his brother had been treacherously killed after receiving surrender. Once, prostrated upon the deck under a gigantic Turk, Decatur fired through his pocket to win free.

During the rest of the month, Prebble battered the town. Near the end of that period he sent *Intrepid* as an explosion vessel, under the command of Lieutenant Somers. For some reason she blew up prematurely, and every man on board was lost.

Within a few years, the valuable experience in action that Americans had gained was showing its worth. As the Royal Navy was supreme at sea, there was little restraint on its activities. American seamen were first impressed in 1798, from the corvette *Baltimore*, off Havana. A number of incidents involved the searching of U.S. ships for deserters, or for war material destined for France. For instance, in 1807, H.M.S. *Leopard*, 50, hit *Chesapeake* so severely, while hunting deserters, that 21 seamen were killed or wounded. Four men were taken off as deserters, though three of these were Americans who had escaped after being pressed into the Royal Navy. Two of them were hanged to intimidate others.

This high-handed conduct brought about a declaration of war by Congress in June, 1812. It was a bold gesture, for the

United States Navy boasted only 16 ships all told—the basis was the group of six frigates. In support were listed a light frigate, *Essex*, 32, two corvettes, 28 and 24 respectively, and two 18-gun sloops, with light craft originally intended for the Mediterranean service. At the time there was no Navy Yard and no dock, which meant careening for hull repair.

There was no national preparation for war; the American seamen were resolute and confident. They had experienced action, their gunnery was constantly being tested, and there was no shortage of recruits. Most ships of the navy were over-gunned—the so-called 44s mounted 54, and *Essex*, rated 32, had 46 guns. However, the poor quality of American-made guns balanced this somewhat. Bursting was not uncommon, and the shot were of light weight.

In addition to her main armament of 24-pounders, *President* mounted 22 42-pounder *carronades*. This was a British gun, first produced in the Carron Iron Works, Falkirk, Scotland, in 1778. As the carronade was short-barrelled, its range was limited, but it did terrific damage at close quarters. Seamen called it "the smasher." Some trouble arose over the earliest type, which did not stand far enough outside the gun port, so that the flash damaged the shrouds; this led to a slight increase of barrel length. Carronades were not listed with the ship's official gun strength, so they represented extra hitting power.

There could be no fleet action, with the protagonists so ludicrously unequal in force; American sources gave the Royal Navy of 1810 a total of 1,048 ships. It was in their extraordinary skill and daring that the U.S. seamen appeared supreme, with remarkable success in single-ship duels. This proficiency was the fruit of constant training. Sail drill, clearing for action, gun drill, were practiced daily; every evening when at sea, the ship beat to quarters, the signal for action. In the frequent big-gun exercise, ammunition was expended freely; on a difficult target, ten shots might be

47

fired to get one hit. Each gun crew had two or three members who were chosen as boarders, to leave the gun on call. These men supported the thirty or so Marines on each ship.

Another great advantage was the independence that had always marked the American seaman—no flogging or bullying was perpetrated, and a good spirit was maintained. Even in the crews' messes of eight men and a boy, any quarrelsome character was squeezed out. If necessary, misfits were grouped in a separate mess. American shipboard conditions were always a temptation for the British seaman.

In 1811, some attempt was made to establish a naval hospital. Previously, from 1798, sick and wounded seamen had been placed in civil and private hospitals, being supported by a voluntary fund. An old shipyard in Philadelphia was converted for that purpose in 1811, though it was very small, with only eight beds. This place was described in 1813 as a wretched hovel, entirely without comfort. It was crammed with patients, totalling 24, and each said to be only gathering strength enough to desert.

Until the 1812 war, British captains had paid little attention to odds, but the Americans were the most formidable enemies that the Royal Navy had ever encountered. This was especially noticeable in the heavy crewing of U.S. ships. For instance, in early October, 1812, when the U.S.S. *Constitution* clashed with H.M.S. *Guerrière,* 38, the 44-gun American ship carried 456 men to the British force of 282 men. In every respect the British vessel was outsailed and outfought. As the ships closed, *Constitution*'s gunnery was superior; her opponent was speedily dismasted, with severe hull damage. Musketry exacted a heavy toll in 25 minutes of close-in fighting, and the final casualty figures were 79 killed and wounded in *Guerrière* against 14 in her opponent.

Later in the same month Stephen Decatur, in *United States,* 44, encountered *Macedonia,* 38. In these two ships, the crews were drilled to perfection, though Captain John

Carter, in the latter, had gained his results with the lash. This duel was another triumph of gun drill. Decatur's broadsides were almost two to one, hitting hard on both hull and rigging, while *Macedonia*, shooting high, hit only the rigging. Her decks were a shambles, but the crew fought like tigers, in spite of appalling losses—104 killed and wounded. Maintop, foretop, and mizzen went overboard, and she sustained more than a hundred hits in the hull. It was all at relatively long range, with no grapeshot or musketry, and, as the British fire was high, *United States* lost only 12 killed and wounded.

This pattern of events endured for almost the first year of the war, much to the consternation of the British authorities. Such skill and energy on the part of the Americans was quite unexpected, and created much anti-Government feeling over this. In fact, the British naval system was extremely lax over precision gunfire, through the technique of getting to close quarters, where rapid gun service counted more than accuracy. Most Royal Navy ships fired practice once a year; some had not done so for three years at the time of the inquiry. A captain's orders, on first receiving his guns, forbade him to fire more practice shots than one-third the number of pieces on his upper deck. Six months later he could fire half the number. In many ships, the guns were never loaded at all in drill, and the time saved was expended in sail-handling and decorating.

It seems ridiculous that the immense naval strength of Britain should be thus set at naught, but the decline of Napoleon after his Russian misadventure permitted the Royal Navy to concentrate more force across the Atlantic. During May, 1813, the blockade of the American eastern coast was completed, and seagoing trade was strangled. A type of fast privateer, with one long gun and light boarding pieces, was produced in great numbers to harass British commerce, but the blockade destroyed that of the United States. This was the weakness óf their naval policy—the lack of a strong defensive force for such a long coastline.

One of the British vessels lying off Boston was destined to sound the knell of American triumphs in the war. *Shannon*, 38, had been commanded by Philip Bowes Vere Broke for seven years. Broke was one of the finest captains in the Royal Navy, and a most proficient gunner, with a theory on horizontal fire. His crew, under almost paternal care, acted like a well-tended machine in Broke's routine of battle training. *Shannon's* guns were carefully zeroed, and their individual characteristics studied. Every morning the crew did 1½ hours' big gun drill, and the same length of time was spent in the afternoon at musketry, broadsword, and pike drill. Both guns and muskets were exercised in target shooting twice a week, with a pound of tobacco for each center shot. Occasionally the captain would call on a particular gun crew to score a hit.

Broke knew that the U.S.S. *Chesapeake*, 38, was fitting in Boston, and he sent in a challenge to Captain Lawrence to meet him at any given bearing. As it happened, the letter miscarried, but Lawrence brought out his ship for action on June 1, 1813. His crew had been paid off, so the frigate was manned with replacements, including a number of foreigners. Nevertheless, they fought well. At 50 yards range, the two vessels blasted each other with broadsides. *Chesapeake's* guns inflicted great damage, but she suffered most, with wreckage thick upon her deck. Within a few minutes, rigging damage caused the American to turn her head into the wind a little. That exposed her quarter, which was instantly shattered, and the two ships ran together. *Shannon's* battered crew lashed the two securely, and Broke led the boarders.

Amid the tangle on deck, an intense, bloody struggle—maindeck men pouring up to fling themselves on the British, the latter blasting volleys of musketry down the hatchways. At the height of the battle, Broke went down with a cutlass wound that left part of his brain exposed, but the wave of boarders pushed on. Fifteen minutes after the first shot, *Chesapeake* struck her colors, with 61 dead and 85 wounded. *Shannon*'s losses were 33 and 50. It was a triumph of discipline and training for *Shannon*, her men not being confused by heavy loss. At the same time, every credit was due to the largely unco-ordinated ship's company of *Chesapeake*; the only fully cohesive force was the Marine detachment, which fought to the last.

Broke was made a baronet for an action which badly shook American morale. At the outset, British seamen had been overconfident, with disastrous results, but the Americans' successes in ship-to-ship actions had bred in them the same defect. Once the Royal Navy had gained the initiative, there was no going back, and the American decline began. Their land actions had been largely ineffectual, so that the Capitol in Washington was burned by British troops. When Napoleon was forced to abdicate in 1814, it was obvious that the whole weight of British arms could be turned upon the United States, so peace was negotiated as soon as possible.

4
Shipbuilding Ventures

During the period of upheaval, an ingenious young American was striving to bring out an effective underwater vessel. Through contact with Joel Barlow, who had been at Yale while Bushnell was experimenting, Robert Fulton (1765–1815) of Lancaster, Pennsylvania, made a detailed study of the *American Turtle*. In December, 1797 he first made contact with the Directory of Revolutionary France, to offer ideas for a "mechanical Nautilus," that could help in the projected invasion of England. After some exchanges, Fulton went to Rouen to build and launch his submarine on the Seine, in July, 1800.

Nautilus was cigar-shaped, 21½ feet long and nearly 6½ feet in diameter. Below the main hull was a secondary compartment acting as a water ballast tank and a keel. There was only a difference of 15 hundredweight between the weight of the submarine and the water it displaced, so *Nautilus* could be submerged to about 25 feet and brought up again, simply by admitting and expelling that amount of water. Pumps for these operations were worked by a hand lever with a pinion and rack, like an air pump. As the cubic content of the vessel was 366 feet, Fulton calculated that the three-man crew should have enough air for six hours. This proved inaccurate; he had not considered that activity by the crew used up more air than if they were passive.

Entry was gained through a manhole in the blister conning tower, which had side lights. A large part of the interior length was taken up by the propelling and steering gear, whose long shafts extended from amidships to the stern. By means of a handwheel and pinion, the drive shaft turned a 4.4 foot two-bladed screw propeller at an estimated speed of 240 revolutions (four knots), with a cruising speed of about half that figure. There was an endless chain running from

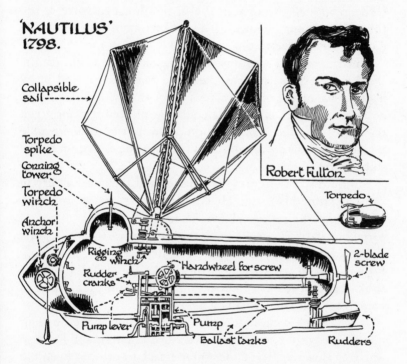

'NAUTILUS'
1798.

Collapsible sail

Torpedo spike
Conning tower
Torpedo winch
Anchor winch

Rigging winch
Rudder cranks

Handwheel for screw

2-blade screw

Pump lever
Pump
Ballast tanks
Rudders

Robert Fulton

Torpedo

horizontal gear wheels amidships to a sprocket on the vertical rudder pivot, for port or starboard movement. An up-and-down travel for the horizontal rudder was achieved with meshed pinions, working from a crank-operated shaft.

Various other cranks projected inside the hull, one for the anchor cable, one to raise or lower the collapsible sail that stood up like half an umbrella for motive power on the

53

surface, and a third to bring up the torpedo. Fulton was apparently the first to apply this name to an underwater weapon. It referred to the electric fish, the *torpedo* or crampfish, which gave a shock to its prey. In this instance, the torpedo was an egg-shaped copper case, with a quintal (100 pounds) of gunpowder. At the front end was a flintlock, which was snapped with a lanyard. A long cable, towing the torpedo, passed through an eye in the threaded spike at the top of the conning tower. This spike was in a sleeve which could leave it fixed in the target.

When in action, *Nautilus* was designed to give beneath the ship under attack, so that the spike could be started in by hammering before it was screwed. In that way the bottom coppering of the ship's hull could be pierced. Having fixed the spike, *Nautilus* was taken on, drawing the torpedo cable through the spike eye, and thus bringing the device up to the ship's bottom.

Fulton displayed great seamanship and technical ability in demonstrating his vessel. He could submerge in two minutes, and he blew up a target barrel in fine style, with a 30-pound torpedo off Le Havre. Though the air supply was not as good as he had hoped, the crew could remain below by candle light for an hour. In an experiment of mid-August, 1800, four men took down a copper globe containing 200 cubic feet of compressed air, and remained below for nearly 4½ hours.

It was some time before the French could make up their minds to engage in what they described as unfair and horrible warfare. However, the underwater attack has always been the refuge of the nation weak in surface power, so in early September, 1800, Fulton was despatched by the French Minister of Marine to prove his theories. He was directed to destroy two British brigs in the blockading fleet, off the Marcon Islands. Fulton's writings on his exploits are very matter-of-fact, but he must have felt something of a thrill as *Nautilus* wallowed over the choppy sea, with darkness around and unknown perils ahead.

At length his night glass picked out the close-reefed topsails of the stationary brigs. A few minutes later the three men were beneath ten feet of water, with the screw handwheel clicking and grinding to thrust them forward. Their exhaled breath condensed on the enclosing shell, so that cold moisture began to drip upon the sweating pair who reared and bent in turn as they heaved around the wheel cranks. With his head in the conning tower, Fulton checked their depth and course with barometer and compass. Though the estimate had been four knots when submerged, it did not reckon with underwater drag, and their progress was so slow that the tide turned while *Nautilus* was still far short. That meant several hours at anchor, with a ventilating tube pushed up to break the surface. Even when they could move with the tide again, they were baffled, for the brigs weighed and moved off. A second attempt made it clear that Fulton's presence was known.

The American was voted 10,000 francs (he had spent 28,000 francs of his own), and promised a bounty for every sinking. He never succeeded in earning it. In spite of perfect demonstrations, and plans for a submarine 30 feet long, with 20 torpedoes, he could never execute a successful attack. It was this lack of effective action that finally set the French against Fulton. His doom was sealed by the appointment of an unsympathetic Minister of Marine, in the autumn of 1800.

Not to be outdone, the inventor followed up his second lead. While the French were considering his offer, in the early part of the year, he had sent a friend, Joseph Gilpin, to approach the British Government with similar proposals. Nothing transpired at the time, but Fulton established further contact after the French fiasco. Having listened to his ideas, including a plan for a surface vessel, the Admiralty's committee of investigation decided in 1804 to finance experiments with Fulton's free torpedoes. These were wooden cases linked in pairs by lengths of rope, each torpedo having a preset clockwork lock. A pair of the destructive agents in action would drift into an anchorage on the tide, catch their connecting line across a ship's cable, and swing in to lie on each side of it, against the hull below the water. Another idea was to send the torpedoes in on "fast rowing boats," to be dropped on each side of the objective. They were connected by a 70-foot line, and the withdrawal of a peg set going the clockwork lock, which in this case ran for five minutes before detonation.

Nothing would go right with Fulton's efforts in actual attack. There were two successive failures when the British sent torpedoes against Boulogne shipping, in early autumn, 1805, yet Fulton blew up a captured brig at the Deal anchorage in a most impressive manner. Fulton's work for Britain was ended by Trafalgar—as there was no French fleet, his weapons were needless. He was paid off with £10,000—a generous sum, considering that his salary had been £200 a month, and that he had achieved nothing for it. No more success awaited Fulton in his own country, for there an antitorpedo defense was worked out by 1810. Chains rigged to the anchor cables and weighted netting suspended from the booms provided an effective means of holding off torpedoes.

Another great Fulton venture was the first effort at a steam warship, the *Demologue*, with a central paddle wheel. It came to nothing, like so much of his work, and it only served to show that the time was not ripe for such an idea. During those early years of the nineteenth century, the sailing ship was approaching that degree of perfection that preceded its decline before the steam boiler. Yet it was only in the last 20 years of the eighteenth century that big ships had generally dispensed with the old lateen yard. By about 1750, the forward end of the lateen sail had gone out, but the long yard remained until after 1780. It was then

56

dispensed with, so that only the after part of both yard and sail continued in use as a fore-and-aft rig. A lower spar known as the boom was provided to spread the foot of the sail, and the yard became the gaff. In the merchant service, the sail was known as the *spanker*, but in the Navy it was the *driver*.

Among merchant ships of the Napoleonic period, the East Indiaman was still supreme, though it was too much like a warship to be typical of a trader. In the largest Company ships, of 1,200 tons, were a number of warship features. They were two-deckers, with naval quarterdeck and poop, though of course the interior layout differed. As the ships had little sheer or curve on the top line, their *floor timbers* (those nearest the keel) were much flatter than normal, with great fullness in the bilge and ample cargo-spaces.

A big Indiaman of that time mounted 56 18-pounders, and the structure was so sturdy that the type was gladly taken into the Navy. David Steele's *Naval Architecture* (1804) gives an excellent specimen of a 1,257-ton East Indiaman, with a close stern having two tiers of windows. There was a round bow built right up to bulwarks level, and a continuous upper deck ran between the quarterdeck and the forecastle. This showed a move from the old-type sheered vessels with high stern structure.

A number of the Company's ships were India-built of teak, which permitted the use of iron bolts. These did not corrode in teak as much as in oak, and the use of iron *knees* (brackets connecting beams with side timbers and planking) was suggested by the Company's surveyor in 1791. Iron knees were used in East Indiamen by 1810.

This was a highly selective line, carrying a few passengers under much better conditions than other ships provided. It meant a high passage rate—as much as £240 for a top-ranking officer. Captains were directed: "You are strictly required to keep up the worship of Almighty God on board your ship every Sunday . . . Be humane and attentive to the welfare of

57

those under your command." Passengers themselves were warned regarding decorum and propriety. They received copies of the regulations governing conduct when they went on board, and it behoved them to co-operate, as the Company had the monopoly of the India Service. That concession was withdrawn in 1813, so the directors had to face competition which resulted in the close-down of actual India trading by the Company in 1833. One surviving East Indiaman, *Java*, built in Calcutta in 1813, was in use as a coal hulk in Gibraltar as recently as 1948. Though much damaged and altered, she still preserved the main features of her class.

It is curious that exact details only of top-class passenger ships and of colliers have been preserved—classes widely separated in function, though the collier was an important class of tradeship. Cook chose that type for his great discovery voyages, partly because he had known it well as a boy, but chiefly for its bluff bows and sturdy design—a style known as *cat-built*. *Endeavour*, the first Cook vessel, was a two-decker with a deep hold, and the deck level of cabins and forecastle quarters was well below the upper deck. This ship was better planned than earlier colliers—she had five stern windows—but Sir Joseph Banks, who sailed in her, would not agree to board another collier for the second voyage.

Vessels like *Endeavour* were rated in the *bark* class, as having no square mizzentopsail. Actually *Endeavour* was ship-rigged, so she had the topsail. Colliers of the nineteenth century were built with two masts, thus becoming brigs. It was not the general practice to rate a merchantman by her rig, until the second half of the century; until then she was described by her build or purpose. As regards ornament, only the biggest ships mounted figureheads, despite their universal use in the Royal Navy.

British shipbuilding tended to be influenced by foreign designs. Numerous improvements in warship lines can be traced to captured French vessels. In fact, during the wars of

58

the Revolution, a number of prizes served as actual models for new English types: This also applied to the fine American frigates. The British warship of the period 1810—1820 had a number of permanent developments in line and in upper works. By 1811, under the direction of Sir Robert Seppings, Surveyor of the Navy, every ship had the rounded bow up to forecastle level. This prevented a head sea from creating such wet conditions in the forecastle as had the old beakhead form, and, at the same time, too, more gunpower was available on either bow. After some transitional designs, the stern was built in elliptical form, i.e., a flattened curve instead of the circular line. More stern chasers could then be mounted.

One of the most important changes was the structure of the "upper deck." Until the second half of the eighteenth century, the waist of the ship had been open in the old style, exposing the deck below. Along the sides, spare spars were laid to allow passage across to the forecastle and the afterpart. On these spars the ship's boats were stowed. Temporary gangways were first arranged in 1744, becoming wider and more permanent a few years later. Additional support by fixed cross beams was provided by 1790, after which an extension of the gangways almost decked in the waist (c. 1820). Boats covered the remaining space. Some large warships did not have this gap bridged with decking until 1832, when Sir William Symons became Surveyor. In these successive moves, the old-time breaks at forecastle and quarterdeck were levelled with the upper deck, though the two sections retained their names.

Symons made sweeping changes in the underwater lines of Royal Navy ships. Until his term of office, the Seppings features of round bows and stern produced stronger ships than before, but they were relatively slow. By designing a hull of much finer section, with steep floor timbers, Symons developed fast sailers. It is true that the fine line created more roll in ships with lower-deck guns, so that accurate fire was more difficult, but in the main, Symons' ships were successful.

From the seaman's point of view, the post-1815 period meant some advantages for those retained in service. One gradually spreading improvement on shipboard was the system of iron tank storage for water, first introduced in 1801. This removed a source of infection that had plagued seamen for centuries—the mushy interior of the wooden water-barrel strakes. Another fundamental change was in the wind. Though little was heard of canned meat on board, there is evidence that at least it was on issue in the Navy. In 1952, a can of meat that had been prepared for Naval stores in 1818 was opened and tasted; it was still edible.

On the other hand, old enemies still endured. Service in the Royal Navy was no longer enforced by the press gang, but it was not limited to a set length. Only decay, incurable disease or death could release the seaman. Men who were invalided transferred to ships on harbor duty, where everyone, young or old, petty officer and seaman, dragged and toiled like convicts. It was possible to transfer back into the Service to escape from harbor duty—in fact, there was no limit to the number of times that a man could be invalided and re-enter service. Though one might buy out of the Royal Navy, it cost £80, man or boy, and this was the most that a seaman could scrape together with the most rigid economy.

In spite of the enlightened example of Captain Cook, scurvy was still a scourge on board. Gunner William Richardson, who left the Service in 1819, had scurvy so badly that his gums swelled over his teeth, and his food was covered with blood as he chewed. When fresh and green food was available, the gums "broke away bit by bit at a time, without any pain as the new ones came."* Richardson noted that a dent made in the flesh with the finger was visible for a

* *A Mariner of England*: ed. Col. Spencer Childers, 1908.

long time, and that a small pimple on the thigh spread until much of the flesh was eaten away.

At that date, the Royal Navy had been cut down to its peacetime strength, from 99 ships of the line and 495 frigates to 13 and 89 respectively. Manpower was reduced just as drastically—of a force of 140,000 seamen and Royal Marines, only 19,000 were retained. With mixed feelings, the rest were paid off—not in cash but, as usual, in notes payable only at the Navy Pay Office in London. Here the seaman had to make up his mind—walk to London from Portsmouth, a distance of 74 miles, or sell his note to one of the numerous brokers at a heavy discount. If he decided to walk, he sought out other shipmates with the same idea, and the group set off with collective defense against robbers en route. It was a common sight on the narrow London road, the band of sunburned fellows with the seaman's rolling gait, marching in their shoregoing rig, a formidable cudgel under the arm and perhaps a cutlass of two among them.

Once the pay was in the seaman's hand—28s. a month for an able seaman, and 19s. for the ordinary grade—his first task was to defend it from the male and female predators of London. Next, his future. He could seek merchant service, or ship across to the coast of Venezuela, where Simon Bolivar (1783–1830), the Liberator, was breaking away the Spanish yoke. Bolivar and his supporters welcomed the trained and battle-hardened British servicemen, and in that furious struggle for independence, the Britons gained rapid promotion.

5
Sail against Steam

While the graceful sailing vessel was attaining her peak of beauty and efficiency, with the science of sail management at its highest level, a dark and sooty offshoot had made considerable progress. In the steamboat, an entirely new type of seaman appeared. His concern was with boilers and smoothly working pistons rather than with towering white pyramids of canvas and the whim of the wind. He was of independent type, the seaman engineer, and above the sneers that saluted frequent breakdowns.

They were small beginnings, those tiny paddle units of the late eighteenth century, but they set going the vast upward spiral of the steamship. If we discount the undeveloped steam tug of Jonathan Hulls in 1737, supposedly tried on the River Avon in Gloucestershire, the last quarter of that century was the age of progress. This was set on by the Marquis de Jouffroy, a noted French technician, with his duck paddle steamer of 1776. It had a single-acting Watt engine, with a separate condenser. A similar power plant was used in the Marquis's improved paddle-wheel vessel, which plied on the River Saône at Lyons in 1783.

Two American power-boat enthusiasts were at work by 1787. James Rumsey of Virginia used water-jet propulsion, with a steam pump that forced out a stream of water astern to give forward thrust. An eccentric Pennsylvanian, John Fitch, expressed his ideas in a 7 m.p.h. 45-foot boat with a high framework carrying 12 oars in groups of three, six oars on each side. By means of long, horizontal cranked rods, the engine lifted each set of six in turn, carried them forward, plunged them into the water and drew them back with a canoe-paddle rhythm. There is no record of the passengers' reactions to the heaving and diving paddle staves on either side.

In 1790 Fitch streamlined his clumsy transmission to produce a three-paddle, stern-driven vessel powered by a two-cylinder beam engine. A crankshaft with wheels was driven off the beam. At the outer hubs of the wheels, horizontal rods described an elliptical movement that raised and brought forward the three square linked paddles, to drop them for the drive back through the water. This steamboat achieved a speed of eight miles an hour, on the Delaware River. It was all so grotesque, and Fitch himself was so wild and excitable, that no public support was given—in fact, people moved off uneasily when the inventor hove up.

Still seeking recognition, John Fitch turned to experiments with the screw propeller in 1796. He tried an 18-foot screw propeller boat on Collect Pond, in New York City, a pond long since drained and built over. These efforts were technically successful, but no one would listen to Fitch's fanatical prophecies of steamships crossing the Atlantic. In despair, he returned to his native Pennsylvania, where he could be seen stalking the streets of Philadelphia, a gaunt, ragged figure, like a symbol of lost hope. In 1798, he drowned himself in the Allegheny River.

On the other side of the Atlantic, the germ of the steamboat was being fostered by the Scotsman, William Symington (1763–1831). His engine was first applied by an Edinburgh banker named Patrick Miller, who had an estate at Dalswinton. Miller had a 25-foot double-hulled pleasure boat in 1788, which he fitted with the two-cylinder engine in one hull, and the boiler, externally fired, in the other. Between the hull were two paddle wheels in tandem.

63

When in operation, the two pistons were connected by a chain which ran over a drum mounted above them, and they turned the drum in alternate directions through the chain. A longer, continuous chain passed over the drum and around loose pulleys on the paddle-wheel shafts. As the to-and-fro of the drum was conveyed to the loose pulleys, teeth on the inner flanges of the latter engaged a ratchet on each shaft, so that a continuous forward turn was achieved. As the overhead drum shaft turned to and fro, a pulley on it moved the weighted rod that worked the valves. On the lake at Dalswinton, the steamboat travelled at 5 m.p.h. It was only employed for a few trips, then Miller had the engine mounted in his hall. At present it may be seen in the Science Museum.

Thirteen years after this experiment, Symington supplied the steam unit for the first commercial steam vessel in the world, the 56-foot tug *Charlotte Dundas*. She was built for service on the Forth and Clyde canal, by order of Lord Dundas, an important shareholder. His lordship named the steamboat after his daughter.

In the new vessel, transmission was badly organized, for the improved 10 h.p. engine was sited well forward, to drive the stern paddle wheel. Much energy was wasted in working the long connecting rod, and the steering was even more remote—a wheel right up in the bows. However, *Charlotte Dundas* performed well on her trial run (March 2, 1802) for she took two barges, each with 70 tons, over a course of 19½ miles at 3¼ m.p.h.

Despite her success, the vessel did not bring a fortune to her designer. He suffered a great disappointment when the death of the Duke of Bridgewater deprived him of an order for eight similar tugs. There then arose the fear that the wash from the tug's stern paddle wheel would damage the canal banks, so she was moored in a side waterway until 1861, when she was broken up.

It is curious that the earliest steamboat builders were

64

running neck and neck on either side of the Atlantic without knowledge of each other's activities. Further developments in America were due to submariner Robert Fulton. While in Britain, he had recorded and sketched in detail the work of Symington, so before leaving the kingdom in 1805 he ordered a suitable 20 h.p. engine from Boulton & Watt. This was intended for his projected vessel *Clermont,* which was built 150 feet long. With her 15-foot side paddle wheels, the steamboat reached 4¾ m.p.h. on the Hudson River in 1807. In the following year, rebuilt and renamed *North River*, she commenced a long period of passenger service between New York and Albany, the fare being seven dollars each way. This was the first regular steamboat passenger service in the world.

Meanwhile, the Scottish enthusiasts were working on another contribution, as the first regular European passenger steamer. She was laid down in 1811 and named *Comet*, with reference to the great comet seen in that year. A hotel owner, Henry Bell, of Helensburgh, Dumbartonshire, commissioned the 40-foot vessel from John Wood's shipyard at Port Glasgow. John Robertson of Glasgow supplied the engine.

Bell's idea was to run a passenger service on the Clyde between Glasgow and Greenock, which service he opened in August, 1812. Though *Comet* changed hands during the following years, she continued at work in the Firth of Forth, and later from Glasgow to the West Highlands. *Comet* was a distinctive craft, with a single tall funnel that acted as a metal mast, carrying a single squaresail upon it.

In 1820, *Comet* was wrecked on Craignish Point, Argyllshire, but by that time three sister ships were in operation—*Elizabeth*, *Clyde*, and *Glasgow*. That little fleet foreshadowed the mighty procession of British steam vessels that would be built on the Clyde. Here was the earliest center of marine engineering, and it still has a high proportion of the world's craftsmen. Writers of seafaring stories are fond of introducing the Scottish engineer.

65

C

Until the early nineteenth century, a seagoing ship's motive power was dealt with by men versed in the craft of seamanship. Sail trimming and judgment regarding weather conditions were essential features of ship management. When mechanical forces were applied, they were the province of a specialist, so that there was a man on board whose knowledge

SEAMAN & BOATSWAIN, R.N., 1828.

of sea lore might be nil. His task would be to keep the engine going, and to maintain the instruments of propulsion. Normally, the engineer would be seen but little above decks, with his greasy garments and black hands.

Quite early in the steamship story a bold attempt was made at an ocean passage under steam. Francis Fickett, in New York, built for Colonel Stevens the full-rigged ship

Savannah, of 320 tons gross and 130 feet in length. She was converted to an auxiliary paddle ship before launching. On May 27, 1819, *Savannah* set out from Savannah, Georgia, to cross the Atlantic. Her 90 h.p. engine was too small, and the coal space was inadequate. Steam power was only employed for about half the voyage, at a speed of six knots, and she arrived in Liverpool, on June 20, under sail.

Though it was not a completely mechanized performance, *Savannah* was the first ship with an engine to make the crossing. Her builder had anticipated only partial use of the engine, so it was arranged that her paddles could be unshipped in half an hour. They were then brought on deck to avoid the drag of the idle blades. An actual all-steam crossing was made by the English-built Dutch vessel *Curacao* (later renamed *Calpe*) in 1827. It was many years before any seaman was bold enough to venture on the crossing without sails as a reserve of motive power.

While the seaman engineer was establishing his importance abroad, the time-honored wooden construction was being displaced. At first the idea of iron afloat seemed ridiculous, until a number of iron lighters (unloading vessels) and barges were successfully worked in 1805. There had been concern for many years over the shrinking of English forest land under the demands of shipbuilders and charcoal burners, but the progress of the miners with the steam pumping engine provided a remedy. Production of coal and iron, the industrial twins, had been greatly increased through the work of Newcomen and Watt on mine pumps.

It would be tedious to detail the progress of iron shipbuilding. Sufficient to say that by 1835 the Scottish builder, Sir William Fairbairn, had moved south to open the first iron shipbuilding yard at Millwall, on the Thames. Iron ships soon displayed their strength in adverse conditions, as with Isambard Kingdom Brunel's *Great Britain*, 3,270 tons, the first screw-propelled iron steamship (1843). She ran

67

ashore at Dundrum Bay, on the Irish coast, in 1846, and remained perched on two separated rocks for 11 months without breaking up. When finally refloated, she was repaired and returned to service.

In September, 1968, the ship came into the news again, when a campaign was launched to bring her back to Britain. She had lain rusting in Sparrow Cove, Port Stanley, Falkland Islands, since 1886; until 1933 she was used as a storage hulk for coal and wool, and in July, 1970, she was towed home to Bristol for restoration.

One of the important changes effected by iron shipbuilding was the changeover in the gauging of size. Wooden vessels had been rated by capacity or burthen in tons, but it became customary to use *displacement* in gauging iron craft—i.e., the weight of water displaced when floating at normal draft gave the rating of the ship.

Our reference to screw propulsion brings us to the third of the great developments in power ships. Early efforts at screw propulsion were hampered by lack of motive power; manual screws produced little speed. A pioneer of the powered screw was Francis Pettit Smith, a farmer of Hendon, Middlesex. His 1836 screw propeller looked like the worm of a mincer, with two complete turns in wood. It was a great success when fitted to a clockwork boat. Smith had a six-ton launch built, with a light steam engine, and as the *F.P. Smith* it ran on Paddington Canal in 1837. During its tests, half its wooden screw broke away under the strain, which instantly increased the revolutions. Obviously, the two-bladed screw thus formed was the more efficient, so the inventor had the two opposed half-turns repeated in metal. Subsequently a company was formed, and the *Archimedes*, 237 tons, with a speed of nine knots, demonstrated the superiority of screw propulsion in 1839. Its inventor was knighted in 1871, for services to shipping.

While Smith was experimenting, the great Swedish

engineer, John Ericsson, was working in England on the same project. In 1836 he patented a contrarotating screw, with two drums bearing helical blades pointing in opposite directions, and revolving on a sleeved propeller shaft. In rotation, the aftermost drum was reversed in direction to counteract the effects of water motion created by the former drum. For the same reason, the after drum revolved at higher speed than its fellow. Ericsson's system was ingenious but unnecessarily complicated for ship propulsion, so he turned with success to conventional screws. Most of his work was done in America, where he went in 1839.

One may see in the nineteenth century story that, at the time when metal and the machine were overtaking the wooden sailing ship, the latter was constantly fighting against competition. Its greatest service came through the work of American designers, whose speedy, fine-lined vessels gained such notice in the Anglo-American War of 1812–1814. Baltimore, Maryland, was the source of a particularly fast schooner type, and its lines appeared in the first true *clipper*, the *Annie McKim*, built in 1832. There was no actual class of ships that could be rated as *clippers*; it was an American term expressive of trim efficiency.

British shipbuilders had never been able to match the beautiful American craft, even though Alexander Hall and Company produced *Scottish Maid* in 1839. She was reckoned to be the first clipper out of a British yard, but nothing at that period could equal *Rainbow*, 750 tons, built in New York. This was an experimental ship, with a length-beam ratio of over 5:1, a knifelike stem, and the fishlike lines beloved of the American builder. When *Rainbow* came *ghosting* across the bay (i.e., making utmost use of light airs) the American seaman was ready to fall to his knees before the sheer beauty of gleaming canvas towering high, the soft murmur of water under her forefoot, and the gracious hull line sweeping aft.

69

It is quite likely that *Rainbow* justified her reputation as the fastest ship in the world, but her speed lines were a death-trap unless the captain could restrain the urge to exploit them. In a vessel of this type, a fair wind and a high sea formed a deadly combination where too much canvas was crowded on. This tended to bow the ship's head, so that instead of riding the waves she cut through them. By taking heavy water over the bow, the ship could sail right under and never recover. On the other hand, an extreme clipper's fine after lines might cause her to be *pooped* or swamped by a high following sea. Almost certainly something of this kind befell *Rainbow*, for she was lost without trace in 1848.

A successor to the champion was being laid down at the time of her end. *Sea Witch*, of New York, was of slightly greater tonnage (890 tons), but in other respects she was a sister ship, with a similar turn of speed. This was constantly in demand, for her notorious captain, "Bully" Waterman, drove crew and ship to the limit. His terrible voice urged the topmen, slipping like monkeys up the shrouds, to greater exertions. In emergency, a lightning decision and instant control of the hands concerned—any doubts or fears among them settled by the sight of the squat, straddle-legged figure, with jutting beard, fixed like a rock on the quarterdeck. Waterman was feared but heartily respected. Though the lash was freely employed, every man knew the captain as a magnificent seaman. He was reputed never to have lost a yard; no sail, or rigging of any importance, had ever carried away, and he had never made an insurance claim for ship damage.

Navigation Acts, the closing of national ports to foreign trading vessels, were a dire restriction on both sides of the Atlantic. When the great gold rush of 1849 brought thousands of fortune seekers to California, they had to sail in American ships, as only these could enter American ports at the time. In this service, Baltimore clippers were employed for rapid passage around the Horn, sailing several points nearer the wind than any other type, and making the utmost of fair conditions. At first it was a one-way traffic, there being no return cargo. After a time, it became customary to make for China and pick up a cargo of tea, rather than to return in ballast (i.e., with a load of gravel to steady the unloaded ship).

In 1849, the British Navigation Acts were repealed, opening British ports to general traffic, so the tea clippers made for London as the best market. *Oriental*, 1,003 tons, ratio 5.7:1, was the first such vessel to unload there, 97 days from Hong Kong. This traffic became a race at the beginning of every season, as the earliest cargoes gained high prices.

American vessels on that run were earning £6 per 40 cubic feet of cargo space, while their British counterparts could only get £3 10s. per 50 c.f. This was a challenge to British shipbuilders. Until 1850 their fastest actual class was the Blackwall frigate, in ratio 4.7:1, which succeeded the old East Indiamen as a standard type. At that date Messrs. Green and Money Wigram, the Blackwall designers, produced the Clipper *Challenger*, 700 tons, at their Thames-side yards. Alexander Hall of Aberdeen built *Stornoway* and *Chrysolite*; the former achieved the fastest passage of 1851 on the England-China run—102 days out, 103 home.

A Liverpool owner, James Baines, who set up the Black Ball line, engaged the great American designer Donald McKay. In 1853 McKay was directed to build four of the finest ships he could produce. His first response was the world-famous *Lightning*, record-breaker of the clippers, though her first voyage was a narrow defeat. *Red Jacket*, of the White Star Line, raced her home. *Lightning* did the best day's run, 436 miles, but her rival made Liverpool from Sandy Hook in 13 days 1 hour, while *Lightning* took 18½ hours longer. Average speeds on this run were 18 knots, it was claimed, but these were probably rarely—attained

71

top figures.

As an emigrant ship, *Lightning* was intended for the Australia route, with first, second and steerage passengers. Those in the steerage took their own bedding, cookpots and food, and they had to fight their way to the galley fire. Even when food was on issue to the steerage, it was so poor and meager that a personal supply was essential. Mortality was high in any case, for if the passage proved rough, the steerage quarters were battened down, creating unhealthy conditions. Captain "Bully" Forbes, with his first mate "Bully" Bragg, took *Lightning* to Melbourne in 77 days (Spring, 1854), and brought her back in a time that has never been bettered by a sailing ship—a shade over 64 days. He is reputed to have clapped the entire crew in jail at Melbourne, on a charge of mutiny, trumped up to prevent desertion.

These high-speed runs were made by means of one policy—"Crack on!" It called for the peak of efficiency in the sail handlers, as a squall when the ship was carrying every stitch of canvas could dismast her. Gymnastic ability, complete disregard of dizzy height, and a high degree of manual dexterity were needed by the seaman whose task was dealing with sail. Up the shrouds like a cat, over the futtock shrouds and out to the yard, scurrying sideways along the footrope below it. Some adepts skipped along the yard itself before getting down to the footrope. It all had to be teamwork. In reducing sail, for instance, some men were unsheeting (casting off the lower corners of the sail). Others, above, hanging arms and shoulders over the yard, were hauling up the canvas to stow it against the yard and secure it with gaskets—short lines attached in a row across the sail, for looping it to the yard. Perhaps in a roll of 30 degrees, the seaman had to cling like a bat, with the heaving deck 150 feet below.

An American merchant commander, Captain Forbes, had introduced in 1841, a most valuable aid to sail handling—the

72

subdivision of topsails on fore, main and mizzen. Donald McKay's *Great Republic* of 1853 was a notable example of the new system, and in 1870 topgallants were similarly divided. By this means a wider range of reefing permutations was possible, and the area of canvas was more manageable. Of course, the actual amount of work was greater over all, and

WATCH ON DECK.
Caulking deck seams.   Sail repair.   Rope splicing.

this was further increased by the staysails between the masts, and the triangular headsails. Inner, outer and flying jibs, with the foretopmast staysail, were designed to prevent a *gripe*, when the ship's head tended to turn into the wind. In fact, that was caused by the pressure of water on the lee bow, though it was not then realized.

On board the racing tea clippers—they were known to

73

c*

seamen as "China birds"—captain, mates and crew had to be a closely knit team. There was a regular supply of prime seamen, not a few being deserters from the Royal Navy on the China station, and crews were usually large. A captain known for his seamanship could man his vessel over and over again. This was so even if he thrashed the ship so hard that the watch feared to leave the deck at the changeover, as with Captain Holmes in *Leucada*.

Throughout the story of the seaman in sail there runs the dark streak of brutal treatment, sadism and mutiny. It is not easily realized that the captain had absolute control over the crew's conditions of life. He was completely master, and any attempt to oppose his will could be rated as mutiny. That was the dread of the afterguard, the ship's officers, so harsh repression was often employed to grind out any such tendency. It was the seaman's part to endure the kick, the lash and the bitter tongue, without daring to look anything but submissive.

Forecastle conditions on the average sailing ship were bad indeed. There was the British "topgallant" forecastle, high in the bows and heavily weathered, or the more comfortable deckhouse type, set abaft the foremast. Often, the seamen made their quarters worse, in the topgallant forecastle. If ventilators were provided, they were almost certain to be blocked up—the hard-bitten seaman preferred a fug to fresh air. Matters were not improved by the stench of beef and pork barrels stowed in the forepeak below, mixed with that of old rope and tar. In all cases, the forecastle was wet, through the position of the hawsepipes in the bows; it was impossible to plug the opening, so the deck was often awash. When hauling in the anchor cable, piles of stinking mud were often stripped off it into the forecastle. Unless the ship was on a tropical run, there was little hope of drying wet bedding or clothes. This could only be done at the galley fire, and the men might be refused the facility to avoid "coddling" them.

74

British ships were notorious for their disregard of seamen's comfort. Board of Trade regulations laid down nine square feet per man for hammocks, and twelve square feet for bunks. Hardly any British forecastles had tables, so the men ate with their plates on their knees or on their sea-chests. Most mess gear was self-provided; it comprised a tin plate and

ROYAL NAVY SEAMEN, 1805.

a shallow pannikin, with cutlery, and a lidded hook–pot for liquids. This pot was like an army canteen, with hooks for hanging it to the bunk side.

As a rule, the shipowners only provided the "mess-kids" in which the forecastle hands' cooked rations came from the galley, and the large wooden "barge" for bread. This was a polite name for the flinty "Liverpool pantiles" or ship's biscuits, full of weevils as always. In spite of the demanding work aboard, many owners seem to have been quite callous about food supplies, buying up scanty stores of condemned Navy issue. This wretched stuff, rancid and half-cooked, would have been refused by any well-kept animal, but it was all that the crew on the high seas could expect.

There was great variety in the sea-chests ranged in the forecastle. Much depended on whether they had been bought ashore or made by the ship's carpenter for sale to the crew. Seamen often spent much time and skill in decorating the chests, with ship drawings and designs inside the lid, and fancy knotwork on the rope handles. By tradition, no chest was locked while at sea, but in port there was no aspersion on one's shipmates if the chest was locked—every port was full of sneak thieves.

When bunks were generally adopted for the forecastle, following the American lead, the bottoms were made of tongue-and-groove softwood, with straw mattresses laid on. Coarse, dark blankets were provided by the men themselves; sometimes the blankets had canvas sandwiched between them as an insulation against cold. It was quite normal to sleep in day clothes—in fact, one of the laws of *Oleron* forbade seamen to undress while at sea. Continental seamen usually undressed to sleep; Frenchmen in particular wore immensely thick red flannel nightshirts.

A great drawback of wooden bunks was that the bottom boards harbored bugs, which were prevalent in the forecastle, especially under tropic conditions. Paraffin was poured into the cracks and lit, as a drastic remedy—old seamen swore by it. Fleas from the Australian wool cargoes were another plentiful source of annoyance.

Whatever the discomforts on board, no complaint was offered by the wise seaman, for the lash was used almost as often in the Merchant Service as in the Navy. When reformers attempted to bring in a system of logging shipboard offenders, and deducting fines from their pay, the captain's outlook was that this served no purpose. They held that money was remote to the seaman, and that the sharp immediate penalty was most effective. From the officers' point of view, a merchant ship took aboard some difficult

"HANDS TO WITNESS PUNISHMENT."

material, amenable only to boot and cat. Some were "packet rats," Liverpool Irishmen or New York dockside toughs; others were non-seamen, hoping to survive the passage to New York, where they would desert.

In Liverpool there endures the legend of Paddy West, keeper of a low boarding house for seamen. West had a system for feeding alleged seamen to the merchant ships in port. On the taproom table he kept a large bull horn, and around this the potential crew member would walk. When applying for a berth, he would claim to have been "around the Horn." A sheaf of faked discharge papers were available, and as soon as the West candidate had been signed on, he passed his sponsor the advance note on his pay. If a group of such shams were all together in a watch, their inefficiency could endanger the ship.

Another common means of manning a ship was the use of crimps. These shore agents *shanghaied* likely men by giving

PRESSED MEN ABOARD AN IMPRESS TENDER, 1805.

them drugged drinks, under whose influence the victims were carried aboard. Once on a ship, and at sea, they could do nothing but submit to the circumstances.

Occasionally, there was a ray of light in the dark prospect of sea service. A few beloved ships were captained by understanding and kindly men, sometimes helped by their wives to make the ship a home. It was not soft conditions that the seaman needed—this idea was an utter failure in *Inchgreen* (1877), where washbasins, curtained bunks, mirrors and crockery were provided. Men who had served one voyage left the ship, taking most of the fittings to pawn. Personal influence was the important thing to keep the men contented; a fine instance was Captain T.Y. Powles, who retired from *James Kerr* in 1902. He was a father to both apprentices and crew, and they became imbued with the captain's love of music and sport. Captain Powles raised some excellent cricket teams! Another immensely popular ship was *Cimba*, under Captain Holmes—seamen would work as dock laborers to be on hand when *Cimba* was signing on her crew.

Music was not exclusive to Captain Powles's ship. For centuries the rousing rhythmic songs known as *shanties* (or *chanties*) were used aboard merchant ships to combine the crews' efforts. These chanties varied according to the task in hand, hauling or capstan work, and the chantyman was a valued crew member. In early clippers he was paid an extra four shillings a month. It was his business to lead and organize the singing so that the pull was the climax of each phrase.

Most chanties date from the nineteenth century— *Shenandoah*, for the long, slow pull, and *Billy Boy* on the capstan. It is considered that the first actual song of the type originated in the early seventeenth century, when English and Dutch were trading rivals. This was *Amsterdam*, or *I'll Go No More A-Roving*. Concerted rhythmic shouting of phrases was done in the previous century, but with no continuous music.

Obviously it was of benefit in working the ship if the men were singing, and it was an ominous feature if they would not. Some traders, like the Blackwall frigates, shipped fiddlers with special duties and extra pay, while Scots vessels would sign on a piper. In the Royal Navy, musicians were aboard, but chanties were not encouraged—in fact, they could be prohibited, in case they made orders inaudible. There were a few occasions on small naval vessels, or when hoisting up big boats, where a "stamp and go" was allowed, such as *What shall we do with a drunken sailor?*

79

At the opening of the Suez Canal in 1869, the death-knell of the sailing ship was sounded. Steamers could cut thousands of miles off the Far East route in that waterway, but its high-level, uncertain winds were useless for big ships under sail. Though many of them, fine, fast sailers, were diverted to the Australia run, with wool and grain, they could not compete with the steamer whose time schedule varied so little. Contrary winds or conditions might throw the clipper weeks out of reckoning over the 10,000-mile voyage.

A foul blot on the use of sail was the unscrupulous insurance of rotten ships, which were then sent out in the knowledge that crew and ship were likely to be lost. There was nothing to prevent an owner from doing this. Some villainous merchants made a practice of buying old ships that were on sale for breaking up. (These would cost about 4s. a ton against perhaps £14 a ton for a new ship.) They would repaint and rename these coffins, and even if reproached by the previous owners, would send them out laden. If the crew rioted over the ship's condition, they could be imprisoned for 12 weeks, with hard labor. An alternative was to send a policeman on board to overawe the seamen who were being sent to death.

Such miserable practices were made public by the Radical reformer Samuel Plimsoll, of Bristol, (1824–1898), who published in 1873 a slashing book, *Our Seamen: An Appeal*. Plimsoll's fiery harangues in Parliament drew great attention. He revealed some of the subterfuges of the coffin-ship owners. They used *devils* (sham bolts, or even boltheads alone) to give an appearance of strength in a rotten ship's structure. By sheer eloquence and sincerity, the reformer succeeded in putting through the Merchant Shipping Act of 1876. It provided Board of Trade inspection of commercial vessels, and the painting of a load line or Plimsoll mark to show the water level to which the ship could be loaded with safety. In this way, the merchant seaman was saved from being sacrificed to greed, and many old sailing ships went to the breaker's yard.

With the decline of sail went much of the picturesque and the traditional in shipboard life—the sailmaker and the caulker, the rigging repair, and the delicate scrimshaw carving

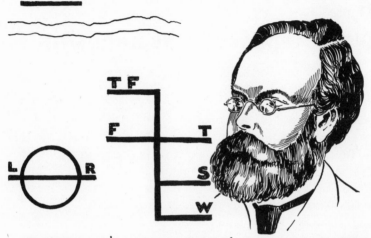

THE SEAMAN'S SAVIOUR: SAMUEL PLIMSOLL, 1824-1898.

of the watch below. However, the balance was struck by the improved general conditions of life on board. Though many sailing ships were built and worked in the early twentieth century, it was a dying race.

81

6
New Aspects of Seamanship

In the seaman's life of the mid-nineteenth century, the keynote was expansion. Sea lore had been unchanged for centuries before the age of steam. Ability to handle, reef and steer, and fight the guns; weather wisdom, the quick reaction in emergency, were the stock in trade. For a long time, the Admiralty was very cautious about the use of steam in the Royal Navy. While paddles remained as the operating gear, steam warships were of relatively small size and power, for paddles were too vulnerable under gunfire.

Nevertheless, a number of such vessels were commissioned, a good example being *Gorgon*, 1,111 tons, a Symons steam paddle frigate, launched at Pembroke, Wales, in 1837. *Gorgon* had the distinction of housing the first direct-acting marine engines. In these, the cylinders were set immediately under the crankshaft of the paddles, so that the short connecting rods drove it direct, with only a short travel. This was far preferable to the older system, where a great part of the energy was spent in moving side-levers and long rods. A rate of nearly ten knots was achieved by the steam frigate.

Soon after *Gorgon* was commissioned, Turkey made a treaty with Britain, Russia, Austria, and Prussia for help in subduing her turbulent vassal Mehemet Ali, Khedive of Egypt. A highlight of the brief naval action in November, 1840, was the siege of the Syrian seaport of Acre. In was held by Egypt at that time, and a British fleet bombarded it for three hours, reducing the town to ruins. This was the first fleet action that included steam warships. *Gorgon* was there, mounting two 10-inch and four 30-pounder guns. *Cyclops*, another six-gun frigate, with three paddle sloops, *Vesuvius, Stromboli*, and *Phoenix*, made up the rest of the British steam flotilla, while the French navy contributed the steam paddle *Magicienne*, 24.

In 1843, an attempt was made to establish a larger type of paddle warship; the frigate *Penelope* was cut in two, lengthened, and fitted with 650 h.p. engines. Though the Admiralty built other ships of that type, it was obvious that the system was inferior in general utility value when compared with the screwship. It was the screw propeller that made the large steam warship a practical affair. A protective housing could be arranged over the screw, apart from its initial concealment in the water. For a time it was a weird combination, the massive full-rigged ship with her black-and-white striped hull and a slender funnel or two sticking up among the standing rigging.

Ericsson's screw propeller was being used in a number of American river steamers, and the screw vessel *Princeton* was built for the U.S. Navy in 1842. British designers had their minds made up by a famous tug-of-war in April 1845. Two steam sloops, H.M.S. *Rattler*, screw, and H.M.S. *Alecto*, paddle, were lashed stern to stern for a test of hauling power. There was nothing to choose in size or nominal horsepower, but *Rattler* towed the other vessel astern at nearly three knots. A point that should be regarded is the difference between *Rattler*'s indicated 300 horsepower and *Alecto*'s 141. *Rattler*'s screw is preserved in the Science Museum, London.

There was much work to be done on hull design regarding steamships. Efforts to convert wooden sailing vessels to steam showed the difficulty of not gaining enough space for engine seating and working, while coal bunkers were always inadequate. Long after the middle of the century, screws were designed to be feathered or unshipped, so that the more familiar motive power of the wind could be used without drag. It was said that sail training was invaluable for breeding resourcefulness in officers and men. For that reason warships were kept rigged long after it had been admitted that rigging impeded the ship in action. A special set of sheerlegs was rigged to raise the screw when sailing.

H.M.S. 'DUKE OF WELLINGTON, 131 GUNS: 1854.

One of the most powerful of the screw-driven "wooden walls" was the *Duke of Wellington*, 3,771 tons, launched at Pembroke in 1852. This vessel was fully rigged, and when fully equipped with stores and gear the total cost was nearly £202,000. Here was seen the multiple broadside battery in its last form—131 muzzle-loading guns on three decks, with the 32-pounders below. Two hundred men worked for a year to build the huge hull, and 24 riggers spent 30 ten-hour days in setting up the tackle. There were 970 men aboard when *Duke* was fully manned, but among the crew there was a sharp cleavage. Gunners and sail trimmers had nothing in common

1845   1854
SEAMEN OF THE ROYAL NAVY.

with the engine room staff, and as the latter were increasing in numbers their significance grew.

At first, the engineer seamen were supervised by their own warrant officers, a concession granted in 1837. Ten years later, commissioned Engineer Officers were appointed, and allowed to wear a distinctive uniform coat—blue, with purple rings

85

around the cuffs. Badges of rank comprised crowns or stars in gold, with silver on the epaulettes. There was nothing to distinguish the engine room crew when they went ashore. They wore the wide canvas trousers and the short, tailless blue jacket, single-breasted, with many buttons, much as their predecessors had done thirty years before.

THE NAVAL BRIGADE:
SEAMAN AND OFFICER, 1854.

However, where the old-time seaman had worn only a shirt under his jacket, *guernseys* (jerseys) were being adopted by the Royal Navy. About 1845 H.M.S. *Blazer* became noted for the gay blue-and-white barrel-striped guernseys worn by the captain's boat crew, so possibly this gave rise to the name "blazer" for a striped flannel sports jacket. Many seamen could make their own clothes, but their pride was the stiff, round canvas hat, glazed with many coats of tar. There was still a fancy for the black kerchief knotted loosely around the neck, though Royal Navy seamen often appear in prints with bare necks and wide collars turned back on their jackets.

From the middle 1840s the loose *frock* (like a baggy

WARRANT
OFFICER, 1863 DRESS   CHIEF PETTY
OFFICER, 1855 DRESS.

jumper) was worn by ratings on the Royal yacht. In summer the frock was white; there was a V-neck and a turned-back blue collar with three white stripes. These stripes were simply a survival of the old taped seams, and they did not signify three famous battles, as some people considered. Bell-bottom trousers completed the kit, with the frock tucked into them to bag out at the hips. Actually, this dress, with a flat, ribboned cap, was the basis of the wretched "sailor suit" into which the Victorian small boy was crammed.

By 1856, the example on the Royal yacht had brought about a report from the authorities on the advisability of uniforms for the seamen. After conference between the

ABLE SEAMAN, 1857:
First official rig.

Admiralty, Naval base commanders and serving captains in 1857, a rig was decreed in 1857 that resembled in many ways the familiar Royal Navy uniform. It included the bell-bottom trousers, and the loose frock with a broad turndown square collar. These items were normally in blue, but the tropical kit was white duck (linen) with a sennet hat (in a type of straw);

88

the latter was covered with black-painted holland when it was worn with the blue rig. A flat blue cap, with a black ribbon, was the usual wear with blue, and accessories were a lanyard with a jackknife, frequently worn at the waist.

In 1863, watch stripes of red were displayed on the upper sleeve, on the appropriate side for port or starboard watch. These stripes were blue on the white rig. At about the same time came the issue of the sleeved flannel vest, which still survives in the Royal Navy. It was then square-cut at the neck, with a binding of blue tape. There still exists a specimen of 1890, the earliest known survival. Another long-lasting order concerned facial hair. For many years whiskers had been permitted, but the beard and mustache had to be shaved. From 1869, the latter appendages were in order, but all had to be grown or none, and permission gained to grow or shave.

This great change, from the wearing of accepted but unofficial clothing to the first regulation rig, was typical of the new era. Seamen beheld the old free-and-easy days receding before mechanization and centralized direction. One unwelcome link remained—the gratings were still.to the fore at "Hands to witness punishment." Admiral Sloane-Stanley wrote of *Albion*, in 1852, that there was hardly a week in which some crew members did not undergo three or four dozen lashes. In most cases drunkenness was the offense— through shore leave, not the rum issue, for the old ration of half a pint of grog daily was much reduced after 1823. Perhaps the boatswain's mates did not lay it on as stoutly as of old, for the admiral never saw any instance of great laceration, and the men did not appear to think the punishment degrading.

That was a period of great difficulty over manning the Fleet. Lord Clarence Paget, commanding *Princess Royal*, 91, wrote of his experiences in October 1853:

"There was a scarcity, indeed, almost an absence of

seamen. However, with the aid of several valuable officers who were appointed to the ship, and by dint of handbills and touting of all sorts, we managed to enter at the average of twenty to thirty a week, such as they were. Scarcely any of them had been in a man-o'-war, and consequently they were entirely ignorant of the management of great guns and muskets . . . I wrote and wrote to the Admiralty, stating that if they did not assist me by placing two hundred coastguards on board, I should be taken by the first Russian frigate we fell in with."

A report from the Committee on Manning (February, 1853) had already established official continuous service (for ten years), with arrangements for boys' training on a larger scale. Pay was still niggardly, which formed the greatest obstacle to recruitment. An able seaman drew 48s. 1d. per month, an ordinary seaman 38s., and a boy, First Class, 17s. 9d. Extra pay was awarded for good conduct badges, re-engagement, and special ratings, so that an ambitious seaman could augment his basic pay a great deal.

Not much improvement in recruiting figures was to be seen by 1859, so a Royal Commission report in February recommended at least five large training ships for boys: more reserves with better gunnery training: more comfort and better food for ratings, and a revised pay and allotment system. In fact, the rates of pay for seamen were the same until the end of the nineteenth century. An Admiralty order of April, 1859, increased the biscuit issue from 1 pound to 1¼ pounds per man per day, and sugar from 1¾ ounces to 2 ounces. There was an extra issue of ½ ounce of sugar and ½ of chocolate to sick ratings, or those on exposed duty.

By the same order, a good deal of kit was on free issue for recruits, or boys becoming seamen. A basic rig of cloth jacket, cloth and duck trousers, serge and duck frock, black silk handkerchief, and shoes could be drawn, or the value in money at £2 12s. 4d. Mess utensils and bedding were free as well. These concessions brought into the service a better flow of recruits. Boys'-training ships were established, and the Corps of Royal Naval Volunteers was raised (later the Royal Naval Reserve, its first commissions being granted in 1862).

In spite of the advance in naval architecture, the mid-nineteenth century was not a period of prominence for the Royal Navy's ships in action. It is true that events of that time brought about another epoch-marking development. This was due to the tension between Russia and Turkey that set off the Crimean War (1854—56). Turkey's decayed political state had led the Tsar to suggest that Britain and Russia should take over Turkish lands to administer them, and help the country to recover. His Imperial Majesty's true intent was to use Turkey as a gateway to India. At the same time, offense was given to France over the Russian occupation of French monasteries in Turkey.

After the destruction of a weak Turkish flotilla by a Russian force at Sinope (November 1853), war was inevitable. A feature of the Russian attack was the use of explosive Paixhans shells for the first time in a major action. By this means the Turkish ships were utterly destroyed, with scarcely any survivors.

In this campaign, which opened for the Allies with a declaration of war on Russia (March 1854), there was much ship-to-shore action. Both Britain and France had strong fleets in the Mediterranean; the former assembled seven ships of the line and seven frigates, but no steamers. One large screw vessel, *Napoleon*, 90, was included among the French force; this comprised nine ships of the line and four frigates.

A rare instance of red-hot shot from a ship was seen when *Terrible*, 21, paddle, blew up a magazine on the mole at Odessa. Further damage was done there by rocket-launching boats with 24-pound rockets. There was a little effective action by Russian naval units, despite the presence of the Black Sea Fleet, including about fifteen ships of the line, with many smaller craft. Most of the ships were in poor condition. They were built of fir, which was perishable and likely to splinter badly when pierced. Just before the war the new ship of the line *Caesarewitch* was sent from the Dnieper through the Mediterranean for the northern route. She was forced to put in at Malta, almost sinking, her hull braced around with cables, and the crew at their last gasp.

Had the Russian Black Sea Fleet been an effective force, it could have entirely crippled the Allied war effort without undue trouble. In the first place, both Allied fleets used their ships of the line as transports. Early in March, 1854, the *Duke of Wellington*, 131, left Spithead so loaded with troops and stores that her lower ports were only nine inches above the water. She was in company with 11 other screw vessels and three paddle warships, the biggest steam-powered force ever to leave Britain.

It was the Allies' plan to ferry troops across the Black Sea for a combined land-sea attack on the formidable fortress of Sebastopol, in the Crimean Peninsula. Lack of information combined with transport deficiencies made the operation difficult. While the fleets were anchored close together, French steamers brought to them a number of troops dying of cholera, from the French center of Dobrudscha (July 1854). Until the end of August the disease raged through both fleets, costing the lives of nearly 2,000 Allied seamen and soldiers.

When that blow had been absorbed, the Sebastopol attack was undertaken. There could hardly have been a worse plan; the troops were to be landed on a coast with no good ports or shelter for the ships in autumn storms. Lack of port facilities would hold up supplies, and in emergency the troops could not be taken off without severe loss. One of the basic causes of this bungling was that the high-ranking officers were all too old for naval warfare under steam. Across from Baltchick Bay to Varna labored the overloaded ships. The French, in particular, were so encumbered that they could not have manned a single gun. On each of their line ships were up to 2,000 troops, as well as the crew of nearly 1,000. Though the Russian admiral pleaded for orders to attack the lumbering vessels, it did not transpire, though he had 15 ships of the line.

An outstanding part was played by the Royal Navy in providing shore batteries against Sebastopol. A Naval Brigade had been formed for land service in the Maori War of 1845, and the Crimean unit was an extension of the idea. Every ship in the British force sent all her Marines save for a few guards, her best seamen gunners, and half her ammunition supply. Altogether 2,400 seamen, 2,000 Royal Marines, fifty shipwrights, 65 officers, and 140 guns were disembarked.

Nothing could equal the energy and skill of the seamen ashore. They dragged from Balaclava a train of munition wagons and supplies, and they built up batteries and gun platforms like magicians. Both Allied armies admired the cheerful resourcefulness, the keenness and the dexterity of the newcomers. It was a new departure for them, and they spared no effort to excel. In an action on the day after Balaclava (which was fought on October 25, 1854), Acting Mate William Hewett, of *Beagle*, 6, disregarded an obviously mistaken order to retreat from his battery, then under Russian attack. He slewed his gun to bear on the opponents' flank, blowing away the parapet in the line of fire, and gave a check which resulted in a Russian retreat.

Hewett's action brought him a commission as lieutenant, and he was one of the group who gained the first Royal Navy Victoria Crosses. Decorated with him were Seamen Reeves, Gorman, and Scholefield, whose rapid musketry from an exposed position beat off an attack on the brigade's batteries at Inkermann, (Nov. 5, 1854), and Seaman Joseph Trewavas, *Agamemnon*, for a sea exploit.

Attacks on the Russian strong points from the seaward side

led to the great naval advance previously mentioned. Defensive firing from the fort was so heavy, with frequent use of red-hot shot, that a system of ship protection was developed. It had been discussed before, in 1834, and eight years after that date Captain Lebrousse planned a layered ship defense, cast iron sandwiched between wrought-iron plates. Colonel Henry Paixhans, the artillerist, devised a similar system. By 1849 there were reports of trials in America, but the armor that was adopted in 1855 was the four-inch single wrought-iron plate proposed by Edward Lloyd, of the Admiralty. It was with this that the first French and English floating armored batteries were protected.

A massive Black Sea fort named Kinburn, on the Dnieper estuary, was the testing-ground for the first armored ship attack. This was one of the earliest all-steam operations on a large scale. Here the citadel was of masonry, with earthen parapets (to muffle the round shot) and outer defenses of ditch and sea. Eighty-one guns and mortars were in position, with all-round command. Ranged before the fort were ten ships of the line, screw-driven, with about eighty other craft, and in the forefront were three French armored units, *La Lave, La Tonnante*, and *Devastation*. These floating batteries were stationed less than 1,000 yards from the fort.

Fire was opened at 9 a.m. on October 17, 1855, and the rolling thunder of contending guns was compared by one observer to the sound of a gigantic locomotive overhead. All the combined fire of the great fleet pounded down upon Kinburn at long range, while from the armored craft some fifty guns were smashing in their 50-pound shot at close quarters. Under the torrent of return fire, the floating batteries suffered no damage. Their wrought-iron plates, $4\frac{3}{8}$ inches thick, were backed by 8 inches of oak.

A report from William Russell of *The Times*, the first front-line news reporter, said of the fort's fire against the ironclads: "The balls hopped back off their sides without

94

leaving any impression, save such as a pistol-ball makes on the target of a shooting-gallery. The shot could be heard distinctly striking the sides of the battery, with a sharp smack, and then could be seen flying back, splashing the water at various angles according to the direction in which they came, until they dropped exhausted.''

By 10.25 Kinburn's guns were silent; the fort had been battered into submission.

When the Admiralty learned of the successful use of ironclad batteries, two British armored vessels, *Erebus* and *Terror*, were hurriedly completed and despatched to the theater of war. None of these floating batteries was really a warship. At best, it was an armored gun platform, which had to be towed in a seaway, as its three knots did not give it steerage way.

Though the Crimean War was chiefly a land conflict, its naval aspects brought a complete change of policy. French designers regained the lead after the advent of British armor at sea. At Toulon a wooden ship of the line was cut down to a frigate and sheathed in 4¾ inch wrought iron. She was launched in November 1859—the world's first armored warship, *La Gloire*. In Britain, where iron merchant ships were fairly common, the Admiralty had not favored iron warships. It was easier for the carpenter to plug a shothole in a wooden ship at sea than to have such temporary repairs effected on a pierced iron plate.

With the use of armor, the outlook was improved, so the first British "ironclad," *Warrior*, was launched in December, 1860. She was 380 feet long, displacing 9,210 tons when commissioned, and reaching 12¾ knots. *Warrior* was an armored iron ship, not a wooden craft with an iron petticoat, like *La Gloire*. At the same time, *Warrior*'s 4½-inch wrought-iron armor belt was backed with 18 inches of teak, and inside that was a *skin plating* of ⅝-inch iron, to prevent splinters or bolts from flying off. This belt, 213 feet long,

95

was placed centrally along the sides, so that unarmored sections at bow and stern were each nearly a quarter of the overall length. In succeeding vessels, the belt ran the whole length from bow to stern. At the outset, the main deck mounted a broadside battery of 36 68-pounders and eight 110-pounders, while on the upper deck were two 110s and four 40-pounders. Through the Admiralty's changed views, the age-old timber trade with Scandinavia dried up to a mere trickle, and, more gradually, the demand for rope and canvas followed suit. Wooden merchant ships were still regularly built for many years, but they, too, suffered a progressive decline.

Though *Warrior* was fully rigged as a frigate, it was the practice for a rigged steamer going into action to take in all canvas. By this means, the use of manpower for sail trimming was avoided. This was another blow at sea tradition, for the skilled sail trimmer had played a vital part in action. Slowly the seaman was becoming a component of a machine instead of a cell in a living organism. Even the gunner was controlled by a heavy pendulum suspended amidships, to indicate when the ship was on an even keel for firing. In close action, Marines were trained to concentrate their rifle fire on the opposing gun ports, each a gap three or four feet square, with perhaps a dozen men crowded around a gun there.

Among experts, the technique of gunnery, unchanged for centuries, was undergoing review. An intensive study of ballistics was developed, concerning both smoothbore and rifled ordnance. A 32-pound Whitworth elongated shot, roughly 12 by 7 inches, had a flat base, slightly hollowed, and a rounded point. It travelled 450 yards in two seconds, under the influence of a pressure in bore of 13½ tons per square inch. Reduced charges were used at close range so that the shot would produce splinters rather than a clean hole. Normal smoothbore charges weighed from a third to half the shot weight.

In 1858, Sir Joseph Whitworth's rival, Sir William Armstrong, brought out at his Elswick factory a pioneer breech-loading rifled cannon. It had a threaded channel through the breech by which it was loaded, and a block containing the vent was dropped into a cavity at the top to close the breech. A threaded breech block, with transverse handles, was then screwed into the channel, securing the vent piece in position. Firing was effected by a percussion tube, which was inserted in the vent and struck by a small hammer operated by a lanyard.

In the 32-pounder Armstrong there was a 10-foot 6-inch steel-lined barrel of 3.27 caliber, rifled with 40 shallow grooves at one turn in 12 feet. This "screw gun" was far in advance of any other weapon of the time. When firing its lead-coated iron shell, with a percussion fuse, a 5-pound charge sent the shell 5¼ miles, and at 1,000 yards it scored 57 hits in succession. It could be served at three rounds a minute, according to report, and the bore was sluiced with water between shots. On shipboard the Armstrong was mounted on a recoil slide carriage; on recoil, it slid to the top of an incline, was checked there for reloading, and released to run down into firing position. Sir William modified the gun in 1859 by using a built-up barrel of wrought iron shrunk on in layers around the steel lining. His original shell casing of lead was reduced to two bands of lead, which gripped the rifling just as well.

In spite of this early introduction of a practical breech-loader, the Royal Navy returned after 1863 to muzzle-loaders, which increased in size and weight. Armstrongs had proved difficult to serve in large calibers, through the weight of the two movable blocks. There was the prospect, too, of damage to the breech when under fire; a jammed block would render the gun useless, whereas muzzle-loaders were much less liable to damage.

P

7
American Tragedy

A pleasant feature of the seaman's story in the mid-nineteenth century was the comradely relations between British and American naval personnel. After the fury and bitterness of the 1812 war, a mutual respect and cordiality developed, such as the example recorded by observers of 1854, during service at Shanghai, in the Taiping rebellion. An accident occurred while U.S. Navy men were firing Fourth of July salutes, and a seaman of H.M.S. *Encounter* lost an arm. At once the officers and crew of the U.S.S. *Susquehanna* and *Vandalia* set in operation a collection which realized £283 for the victim.

Service in the U.S. Navy still maintained many of the commendable features noted in earlier days, though it had been under fire from the public. It happened that the author Herman Melville did 14 months' service between 1843 and 1845. His subsequent book, *White Jacket* (1850), was severe on the matter of treatment aboard. Flogging was then a part of the system—certainly a change from the easy officer-crew relationship that formerly obtained. Melville recorded 163 floggings, though these were limited, by regulations, to 12 lashes in each. case. At the time of publication, a bill to abolish naval flogging was before Congress, and, amid strong expressions of public feeling, it went through.

A great drawback of the U.S. Navy was the slow promotion of officers. As there was no retirement limit, lower officers and midshipmen were kept from advancement.

98

This led to degeneration of spirit and morale, especially among the midshipmen. One outstanding officer at this period of U.S. Navy history was the "Cast-iron Commodore," Matthew Galbraith Perry, or "Old Bruin" (1794–1858). He was a man of tremendous enthusiasm and dogged perseverance. When the naval gunnery school at Sandy Hook was opened in 1840, he introduced the big-gun principle into American warships. This was a reflection of Perry's interest in the Paixhans shellfire experiments, which he had seen. It was not a popular idea. Captain Parker of *Columbus* said in 1842 that "the shells were a great bother. They were kept in the shellroom quite sacrosanct, and no one must even look at them."

Perry's idea was a main battery of ten large-caliber shell guns, which armament was mounted on the screw warship *Princeton* of 1842. It led indirectly to a shocking tragedy in February, 1844, when *Princeton* was going up the Potomac River. On board were numerous politicians—the Secretary of State and the Secretary of the Navy, with a number of Congressmen. A huge 12-inch wrought-iron gun by Ericsson was mounted on the quarterdeck, and a 13-inch weapon, called "Peacemaker," and made by Robert F. Stockton, was on the forecastle. During a firing demonstration, with 50-pound charges, Stockton's gun blew up. It killed the Secretaries, and three Congressmen, besides wounding several bystanders. This led to a breach between Stockton and Ericsson, for the latter refused a request to say that the burst gun had been satisfactory in design. It was, in fact, weak behind the trunnions; Ericsson's own gun had been so, but he shrank a number of wrought-iron bands, 3½ inches thick, around the breech. Stockton, in revenge, blocked the payment of Ericsson's account with the U.S. Government, so Ericsson swore never again to work for that body.

There was little action for the U.S. Navy during the 1840s. While the Mexican War (1846) was going on, warships did duty as transports, but as Mexico had no navy, there was nothing to prevent free access to the coast. Commodore Perry was constantly pressing for more thorough training, with training cruises for both midshipmen and seaman-apprentices. Despite the turmoil on the first cruise, resulting in three executions, further pressure brought the development of an old army fort at Annapolis as a naval school (1845).

A remarkable personal achievement was Perry's expedition to Japan, in 1853. Japan was then a medieval feudality, with a social system quite out of touch with the times. No foreign country was permitted access to Japanese ports, except that a Dutch vessel made a call at Nagasaki once a year to bring off any shipwrecked seamen.

After two years' preparation, Perry took a squadron of five ships to anchor in Yedo Bay (Tokio), in July, 1853. He cleared for action, but no hostile move was made on shore, other than a parade of matchlock men. When the port authority's boats came out, Perry demanded top-level contacts, as he carried a letter to the Mikado (Emperor) from the President of the United States of America. Though the Governor was shown the letter, in a highly decorative box, with gifts typical of western civilization, Perry would only surrender it to a prince of the third order. A six-month time lag was agreed, after which Perry should return for the answer.

During the interim, the Mikado conferred with his Shogun (chief minister), and the latter advised acceptance of the foreigners, to gain information. When they had been used in that way, they could be thrown out. Perry returned in February 1854, with seven ships, to receive the concession of two ports open for trade. This enforced contact with the West had dire results in later years.

Toward the end of the 1850 decade, when the bitterness of the southern states was boiling up to active hostility, the

United States Navy was poorly placed for effective action. President Buchanan's Navy Secretary, Isaac Toucey, favored the Southern cause, so he arranged for the fleet to be scattered so widely that scarcely three could be assembled on call. There was a sharp division among naval personnel. A strong Union feeling among the ratings was countered by the fact that a third of the officers from Annapolis (in Maryland) went south to their own states. Some prominent families with a great naval tradition were divided within the family—the Porters, for instance, whose seafaring connections dated back more than a century.

By December, 1860, the Southern states had declared for secession from the Union, to form their own government. This was ruled unacceptable by Congress, as it rendered inapplicable the term "United States." It is curious that, in spite of naval weakness, the first shots of the devastating Civil War were fired by Southern ships, in the anchorage at Charleston, South Carolina (April 12, 1861). A garrison at Fort Moultrie, on the mainland, was commanded by Major Anderson, who became uneasy over the possibility of attack by Southern enthusiasts. He moved to the island stronghold, Fort Sumter, in the bay, where he could reckon the surrounding water among his defenses.

After several months in Sumter, Anderson became short of supplies, so he conveyed a request to Washington. President Abraham Lincoln telegraphed Jefferson Davis, elected president of the Confederate Southern States, to inform him that a supply ship would be sent to Sumter at once. Almost immediately, a number of armed Southern ships made for Sumter and opened a heavy fire, which endured for 36 hours. During the attack, Lincoln's relief steamer hove up, but her captain hurriedly put about and retreated. That small island fort was surrendered after the 1½ days' battering—a relatively small incident which was to prove fatally significant.

A declaration of war by Congress, on April 15, was

followed by a large-scale blockade of Southern ports. In spite of the widespread dispersal of Federal (Government) warships by Buchanan's officials, Lincoln's own Navy Secretary, Gideon Welles, had each Southern cotton port covered by an armed ship before the end of July. He brought up a mixture of craft, tugs, sailing vessels, anything capable of mounting a big gun.

RATINGS, U.S. NAVY, 1861.

These makeshift blockade forces were manned by a great number of volunteers, merchantmen officers and ratings, rather like the naval reserve of later days.

Little, if any, difference existed between the rig of volunteer ratings and those of the regular Navy. A rating was issued with clothing basically like his British counterpart— blue woollen frock, with collar and cuffs of white linen or duck, and blue bell-bottoms. There was a blue lining to the collar and to the breast of the frock, both being stitched with white thread. Cold-weather wear comprised a blue jacket and trousers, a blue vest, and a black kerchief. Black shoes were on issue, and the summer rig replaced blue with white. In all cases the cap, black or white, was flat, with slightly stiffened edges, and no peak.

When war began, the U.S. Navy consisted of 76 ships all told—sailing ships with 8-inch shell guns supported by 32-pounders, and steam frigates and sloops. By 1865, there were 600 warships on strength. In the South there was nothing that could be called a warship, but a slow build-up was effected, so that at its peak in 1864, the Confederate navy mustered 67 ships of various types. Both sides employed a mixture of artillery—rifled and smoothbore, shell and round-shot guns.

Most naval actions were fought in or off the long sounds and inlets that abounded along much of the southern coastline. These engagements proved that it paid to bring by water big guns which could outrange and silence the shore defenses. In some cases landing parties did serious damage to Confederate supply sources; the destruction of salt mills, for example, hampered the bacon and ham curing processes, and contributed to the food shortage.

Shortly after the outbreak, a chain of events began which led to the most famous naval combat of that time. We have already seen the embarrassment caused where Government forces were stationed in the south at the time of the secession. Captain Charles S. McCauley was in Virginia, commandant of Norfolk Navy Yard, on the Elizabeth River, a tributary of the James River. He was disturbed by threats from the government of Virginia, so he decided to burn both stores and ships, including the new 40-gun steam frigate *Merrimac*, 272 feet, 3,500 tons. In fact, *Merrimac* was burned to the water's edge, but she sank before her engines and lower hull could be affected.

By the end of May, 1861, Southern industry had raised the half-burned hulk. It was then built up with pitch pine 20 inches thick, and covered with 4-inch oak to form a floating battery, the barnlike sides sloping at 35°. Over all was secured a layer of 2-inch rolled iron strips, 8 inches wide, running fore and aft. Another similar layer was then riveted on at right angles, and the pilothouse forward of the central smokestack was armoured like the casemate itself. Each end of the latter was rounded, with a 7-inch rifled pivot gun mounted there. Two rifled 6-inch and six 9-inch Dahlgren guns formed the broadside battery. All these were shell guns. An overhang both forward and aft carried the ship's plating about two feet below the water, and at that level a cast-iron ram was attached to the bow.

This ironclad was a combined effort. John L. Porter, Confederate Navy Constructor, made a model based on the rough drawings of Lieutenant John M. Brooke, formerly of the U.S. Navy. Porter supervised the wood building, after which Lieutenant Brooke dealt with the plating and the heavy batteries. Though efforts were made to rename her *Virginia*, everyone still called her *Merrimac*.

Almost all the crew were volunteers, with little knowledge of ordinary seamen's duties aboard—hardly more than 30 of her 320 men had any considerable experience. There had been no exercises, the engines had not been run, neither had a single gun been fired by the crew at the time of sailing, on March 8, 1862. When *Merrimac* lumbered out of Elizabeth River, it was obvious that her engines were inadequate, giving only five knots. With her length, and the 22 feet depth of underwater hull, this speed barely gave steerage way in the narrow, difficult channel. Her captain, Franklin Buchanan, was really unfit for duty, through nervous prostration, but he remained in command. Inside the ship, her crew were confronted with a new aspect of the seaman's career, just as were the French seamen at Kinburn six years before. Where formerly they had peered through the gunports from the lower deck; they now looked out from a casemate 170 feet long, masked with iron and proof against any shot they were likely to encounter.

News of the Southern experiment had already reached the opposing forces, but little regard seems to have been paid. In fact, Federal seamen referred to "that old Secesh curiosity." Ironclad vessels were not new to America. Pook, the naval constructor, had previously built some vessels of that kind, on the design of James P. Eads. These examples, called "Pook's Turtles," were plated on the forward half of the hull.

As *Merrimac* emerged on the James River, she was attended by the partly-armored steamer *Yorktown*, 12, and two small gunboats. In the misty morning light the little flotilla slowly clanked its way toward the Hampstead Roads anchorage, where lay the frigate *Congress*, 50, and the sloop *Cumberland*, 24. A small Federal gunboat, *Zouave*, came up to begin the engagement with her 32-pounder Parrott, and shortly afterward *Cumberland* opened with a heavy pivot gun. Those shots were completely wasted.

Meanwhile, *Merrimac* came on, dark and forbidding, a slow, inexorable advance. Both ships plied her with broadsides, but there was no effect, and at 2.30 p.m. the ironclad opened fire with her forward gun. When she was right upon the others, a broadside of shells crashed into *Congress*, while the ram was driven into *Cumberland*. In going astern to free the ram, it became detached and stayed in the stricken vessel. Aboard her the crew wrought like heroes under a tornado of shellfire. More than a hundred casualties were suffered in five minutes. On decks that were awash with blood and strewn with fragments of humanity, the devoted survivors hoisted their wounded on to racks and sea chests to keep them above the rising water. Despite their hopeless position, the Federal seamen ran up the red "no quarter" flag, to imply a fight to the end. It came when

105

Cumberland sank on an even keel, with her mastheads still above water, and over a hundred men drowned below decks.

Congress was run ashore, under cover of the batteries there, but these could not keep off the terrible attacker. Again and again the stranded vessel was raked from end to end, making of her a blazing shambles. At length *Congress* struck her colors, but the Confederate gunboats could not face the shore fire to take her over. During the devastating action, three Federal frigates, *Minnesota* and *Roanoke*, steam, and *St. Lawrence*, sail, came up the river, but, strangely, they all ran aground. These, with *Congress*, lay under heavy fire until seven that evening, when *Merrimac* returned in darkness to her moorings nearby.

Grief and apprehension were widespread among the Northern forces that night. Their dead numbered 250, with wounded making nearly double that figure, while the attackers had suffered but 21 killed and wounded. *Merrimac* had undergone no material damage, though every exterior feature had been torn away by the storm of round shot, and two guns had been hit in the muzzle.

While yet the Northerners were mourning defeat, relief was approaching. At the time when *Merrimac* was fitting out, the Federal authorities learned of this and advertised for ironclad designs. John Ericsson, forgetting his wrathful vows, submitted the successful plans, based on his early ideas of 1820. He had observed the seaworthiness of Swedish lumber rafts, and he combined this with the turret devised by the American Theodore Ruggles Timby in 1841. It was Captain Cowper Coles, of the Royal Navy, who fitted a revolving turret upon a raftlike vessel in 1859, though it was never fully tested.

At the end of October, 1861, Ericsson's ironclad *Monitor* was laid down in the shipyard of Thomas F. Rowland, at the Continental Iron Works, Greenpoint, Long Island. It was launched 100 days later, on January 30, 1862. *Monitor* was

172 feet overall by 41½ feet beam by 11 feet 4 inches deep, with two feet of freeboard. Amidships was a turret 9 feet high by 20 feet diameter. Her main hull armor comprised five one-inch layers of iron, and the underwater part sloped away sharply at 35° to deflect shot.

An overhang at bow and stern protected *Monitor*'s anchor, screw, and rudder. Amidships was the turret, power-turned on a smooth bronze ring, with hemp packing as a water seal. Around the turret, armor-plating ranged from 8 inches to 11 inches of iron. A pilothouse on the foredeck was heavily

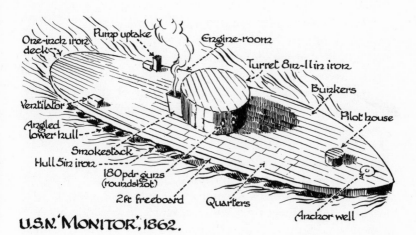

One-inch iron deck

Pump uptake

Engine-room

Turret 8in-11in iron

Bunkers

Ventilator

Pilot house

Angled lower hull

Smokestack

Hull 5in iron

180pdr guns (roundshot)

2ft freeboard

Quarters

Anchor well

U.S.N. 'MONITOR', 1862.

protected, with a movable iron top 1½ inches thick. In all, the ship cost $275,000.00.

All early ironclads had teething troubles, but *Monitor* had more than most. Her trials of mid-February were most discouraging. None of the picked volunteer crew could operate the ship's instruments; the turret worked poorly, ventilation was bad, and the rudder was defective. Ericsson worked on these items, and the two 180-pounder Parrott round-shot guns were mounted on March 4. There can have been little time for the crew to get used to them, for the ironclad was towed out to sea two days later, en route for the South. Lieutenant John L. Worden was in command.

A nightmare voyage followed. *Monitor's* design was only suited to inland waterways, and when rough weather came up on the second day, torrents of water went below through the leaky hatchways. Some waves broke right over the pilothouse, throwing down the helmsman, and the packing around the turret ring was washed away. Water seemed to be pouring in everywhere—around the turret, in at the hawseholes, and down the six-foot smokestack into the boiler fires.

There were steam pumps capable of expelling 2,000 gallons a minute, but the output was only four feet high. Water was pouring down into the blowers, so the driving belts were slipping, while the hand pumps were not strong enough to force water to the top of the turret, the only clear point. As the blower gear was hampered, there was no draught to the fires, and the water in the fire bays filled the engine room with gas. Those engineers who ventured in to check the water inflow were dragged out, choking.

A bucket chain was organized to throw out the incoming water, but the ship was rolling so badly that most of the buckets slopped out their contents en route Steering became a problem, too; the wire wheelropes slipped off their drums, so all hands were put to hauling the ropes under direction. By the morning of March 8, when the vessel reached smooth water, everyone aboard was exhausted, but the day was spent in repairing damage. At nightfall, *Monitor* was in the James River, anchored beside *Minnesota*.

Next morning—Sunday, March 9—*Merrimac* advanced on *Minnesota* at 8 a.m., so *Monitor* went out to meet her opponent. Lieutenant Worden was in the pilothouse, manning the two observations sightholes, with the pilot and the quartermaster. In the turret, Chief Engineer Stimers commanded 16 men, with Acting-Master Stodder at the
108

wheel that controlled the turret movement. Throughout the ship, the other 36 seamen were at their various stations.

When the two champions opened fire, there was no visible sign of the hits they scored on each other. Over the morning stillness of the river, the harsh bellowing of great guns was an offence, like their gigantic volumes of rolling smoke. In *Monitor*'s turret, Stodder was knocked out where he was leaning against the side when a shell struck the turret. Worden came in to ram, but he missed, scraping along his enemy's side. At close quarters his guns drove in a section of her plating several inches. This blow knocked down the crews of *Merrimac*'s after guns, who lay bleeding from nose and ears.

Another discharge at the same point could have pierced the Southern ironclad's defenses, but it was difficult to do this. *Monitor*'s turret was stiff in beginning a turn, but once on the move it was difficult to stop it, so the gunners had to fire while turning. After a short time in action, they lost all sense of direction. Though white lines had been painted on the deck of the turret as a guide, these became black very quickly, and the dizziness caused by turning in the dark confused the men. It was only when the shutters were slid back for the guns to be run out that the crews could see at all, in the few inches of space around the gun barrels.

A great hazard was the impenetrable smoke, which created the danger of firing into their own pilothouse. There had been a speaking tube between the two points, but that was soon broken, and verbal communication by messenger was uncertain and perilous. Over all was the physical effect of being under fire. *Merrimac*'s projectiles being all shells, the Federal seamen had those detonations to bear as well as the discharge of their own guns.

Each vessel's tactics were peculiar to itself. *Merrimac* took 15 minutes to go about and bring her second broadside to bear, while *Monitor* spun like a top. When the Southern vessel tried to ram, her nimble opponent simply skated aside, and in passing she delivered another of those crushing close-range blows. Iron and wood were beaten in, but the shot did not penetrate because the powder charge was restricted. Only 15 pounds were used, instead of the 50 that the great shot needed. Strict government orders controlled this—the bursting of the great Stockton gun 17 years before had imposed caution in using big new guns.

Monitor fired once in eight minutes, but *Merrimac*'s broadside fire gave her two shots for one. Two hours went by, and *Monitor*'s turret ammunition supply was exhausted. It was passed into the turret through a trunk from below, but the turret had to be revolved until a trap in the deck aligned with the trunk. For this reason the Federal vessel had to withdraw while the operation, which took 15 minutes, was performed; she then bore up again. Lieutenant Worden was in the pilothouse at the one-inch sightholes when a shell struck only a foot or so away from them. He was fearfully injured, with burning powder driven into his eyes. At once Lieutenant Greene took over, but there was some confusion, and *Monitor* drifted unchecked across the river. When she was under control again, at noon, she advanced upon *Merrimac*, firing. However, the latter moved off, and returned to her yard to refit.

These redoubtable vessels never met again in action. At the time, each side hesitated to expose its only effective armored unit to possible destruction, and when others were built the original ironclads ceased to be important. In any case, both were out of action within two years. Norfolk Yard was abandoned by the Confederates in May, 1863; they set *Merrimac* on fire, and she blew up. Seven months later, *Monitor*, under Commander John P. Bankhead, sailed for Beaufort, North Carolina. In a violent gale off Cape Hatteras, *Monitor* foundered, but her companion steamer, *Rhode Island*, rescued many of the crew.

110

8
Battle between Brothers

While the Confederate forces were at work with the ironclad system, they were negotiating with British shipyards over the building of fast blockade-runners and commerce destroyers. These were sent out from the yards without guns, to avoid the appearance of British intervention, but Confederate ships met the new vessels at sea and equipped them. *Florida*, built in Liverpool, was the first. She was completed early in 1862, and armed at sea with two rifled 7-inch and two smooth bore 6-inch. After a successful career, she was taken in the Brazilian port of Bahia in October, 1864.

Though six vessels were supplied to the South by Britain, the most famous was *Alabama*, a sail-and-steam sloop on Royal Navy lines, with a hoist-up screw. She made up to 12 knots under sail, and 15 when combined with steam. *Alabama* sailed at the end of June, 1862, under Captain Raphael Semmes, with a crew of 149 including many Englishmen. Her guns comprised a 100-pounder Blakely, one eight-inch shell gun (a 74-pounder), and six long 32-pounders. Like *Florida*, she lasted for two destructive years, before being trapped by the Federal sloop *Kearsarge* in Cherbourg, where the raider had gone to refit.

Kearsarge mounted two 11-inch pivot guns, a rifled 30-pounder, and four short 32-pounders. She was a trifle faster than her opponent, and about fifty feet of her sides, over the engines, had a protective layer of chains between one-inch deal boards. Had *Kearsarge* entered the anchorage at

Cherbourg, international law would have kept her there for 24 hours after *Alabama* had left, so the Federal warship anchored outside to wait. Captain Semmes wished to fight *Kearsarge*, so he went out just before 11 a.m., on June 19, 1864.

For a short time the two ships circled, while the shores and cliffs became crowded with spectators. It appears that *Alabama*'s crew were popular with the Cherbourg citizens. They could distinguish the Southerner by her black smoke—she used Welsh coal, while *Kearsarge* gave off lighter smoke, from Newcastle coal.

After preliminary moves, the combatants closed to 600 yards, and fired furiously. *Kearsarge* made good practice, with over 160 hits for 173 shots, but her adversary scored with only 28 for 370 shots. At noon *Alabama* struck her colors, and after a brief confused exchange of fire, she began to sink. Federal boats then went out for survivors. This was one of the last ship-to-ship engagements of the war, the remaining naval expeditions were chiefly coastal attacks and river gunboats' actions. *Alabama* was the subject of a damage claim by the United States against Britain, as having supplied the raider vessel to the South. In 1871, an international court at Geneva upheld the claim in the sum of $15,500.00.

One of the greatest ship-to-shore naval affairs was the attack upon New Orleans, Louisiana, in mid-March, 1862. It was directed by Captain David Glasgow Farragut, the swashbuckling swordsman-commander. He had been commissioned in 1821, since which time he had gained a reputation that drew the respect and liking of his seamen.

New Orleans was defended in depth. Her forts, Jackson and St. Philip, were many miles downriver from the city, and between the two points lay a fleet of ironclads and gunboats. In addition there were two floating batteries, one of which, *Mississippi*, 16, was reckoned as the best fighting unit in the world. Across the river lay a 40-foot-wide raft boom, held by iron cables and 30 anchors. Though floods had washed a gap in that formidable defense, the gap was filled by eight blockships, linked with chains. Next to the barrier was a flotilla of flat-boats, loaded with pine knots ready to be set on fire.

Against these massed defenses, Farragut brought a force of relatively light craft—one frigate, four sloops, twelve

DAVID FARRAGUT

gunboats, and twenty mortar schooners. Each of the latter carried a 13-inch mortar and two long 32-pounders. When these vessels were anchored in position, Farragut had their upper masts and rigging camouflaged with greenery, so that the outline was lost against the trees behind. Fire from a mortar vessel was a highly developed exercise in gunnery. There was no barrel drag as in a gun, the muzzle velocity was low and the trajectory high, so that remarkable accuracy was

113

possible. As the mortar shell was still a simple cast-iron globe, a length of fuse was cut for it according to the range, so that it burst on target and not in the air. For instance, a 13-inch shell fired at 1,000 yards would need about 1½ pounds of powder and a fuse of about 1¾ inches.

In order to adjust the direction of fire, a *spring* was attached to the anchor, as well as the normal cable. This spring was a secondary cable which was passed out through an afterport and then forward to the anchor. By hauling in the spring on the capstan, the stern of the vessel could be brought around as needed. It fell to the mortar ships to open the action. They each fired once every five minutes, at cost of immense exertion by the mortar crews. There was an acute discomfort as well; the concussion was so terrific that the men ran aft with their mouths open at each discharge. Within a short time every man was black with powder smoke from head to foot.

While this was going on, with cold and red-hot shot thundering from the forts, an ineffectual fireboat attack was launched upon the Federal force. As soon as blanketing mortar fire had beaten down the forts sufficiently, Farragut rammed and broke the raft boom. Having penetrated both active and passive defenses, shattering fire power could decide the issue. On March 28, the forts surrendered, and next day the city followed suit. In spite of the immense volume of gunfire on each side, casualty figures on both sides were amazingly low for eleven days' fighting—Federal attackers, 37 dead, 147 wounded: Confederate defenders 12 and 40.

Farragut was commanding as Rear—Admiral when he fought the action which finally put out of service the Confederate Navy. This engagement took place in Mobile Bay, Alabama, in early August, 1864. Two powerful forts guarded the entry, and underwater hazards comprised 46 lager kegs full of gunpowder. Each had four or five rubber-tube projections, containing glass phials of sulphuric acid, surrounded by chlorate of potash and sugar. When a vessel struck one of these primers the glass broke, and the mixture of the three components ignited the main charge. In addition to the chemical "torpedoes," 134 of mechanical type were strung across the bay entrance. These were like truncated tin cones; a vessel in collision knocked off a cast-iron cap and tripped the trigger below it. Further defense was provided by the ironclad ram *Tennessee*, which was drawn across the fairway inside. She was unusual in that her casemate was lined with netting to protect her crew from splinters.

In the attack, Farragut led the way aboard his flagship *Hartford*, supported by two Ericsson-type monitors *Tecumseh* and *Manhattan*, each with a pair of 15-inch guns carrying 440 pound shot by 60 pounds of powder. Behind the monitors came two Eads turtle-back ironclads, *Chickasaw* and *Winnebago*, with twin turrets mounting 11-inch guns in pairs. When Farragut was advised of the underwater menace, he is said to have replied with an oath and an order for full speed. He crossed the torpedo line safely, but *Tecumseh* struck and went down at once, taking 93 of her 114 seamen. *Tennessee* was pounded by *Manhattan*, while *Chickasaw* lay astern to deliver fifty 11-inch 135-pound shells, after which the Southern vessel surrendered.

Over a hundred years after the taking of Mobile, there was a most interesting sequel. In February, 1967, it was announced that *Tecumseh* had been found at the bottom of Mobile Bay, and plans were made to raise her for exhibition in the Smithsonian Institute.

There is a well-worn saying that history repeats itself. It has done so several times in one respect—the use of the submarine by combatants weak in surface warships. In 1775 the *American Turtle* appeared; the French tried Fulton's *Nautilus* in 1800, and Confederate forces of the Civil War used similar devices. A notable effort in 1863, was the design of Dr. St. Julien Ravenal, a physician, formerly of Chicago. Dr. Ravenal's submarine was 50 feet long, cigar-shaped, and plated with iron. Nine men were aboard the manually driven craft, whose purpose was to break the blockade of the Charleston anchorage.

As it was for attacking "Goliath" (the Federal forces) the doctor named his submarine *David*. It was reckoned to do four knots, with two horizontal rudders to steer her below, or to surface. *David*'s offensive weapon was a *spar torpedo*—an explosive charge rigged on an underwater boom standing out from the attacker's bows. When brought into contact with the objective, the charge was exploded through a wire from a battery box in the carrier craft.

In this case the target was *New Ironsides*, a huge frigate-style ironclad of box-battery type, reputed the toughest in the Federal Navy. She had fired more shots and taken more hits than any other ship, and her plating had never been penetrated. While approaching her at awash level, the submarine was subjected to heavy fire, but the torpedo was exploded against the ironclad's underwater plating with crippling effect. That success was never repeated; none of the other *Davids* was very effective, but experiments continued. *Intelligent Whale* was the incredible name of a Southern manual diving boat, 26 feet by 9 feet. At a demonstration, *Whale* dived in 16 feet of water, carrying an officer in diving dress and two ratings. By means of an escape lock, the officer emerged to fix a torpedo under a target vessel.

These submersible craft were all hand-driven, but a report in the *Illustrated London News* of early 1865 described a powered submarine. At Mobile, in August, 1863, said the report, the Federal *Tecumseh* "was attacked by a torpedo diving boat, with a steam engine and screw propellers, and with two vanes like the fins of a fish."

Spar torpedoes were used on occasion by surface vessels,

but this was a desperate course, involving a bold advance under fire. An outstanding feat of this kind was that of Lieutenant William Cushing, of the Federal Navy, in October, 1863, when he was 21. A Federal position on the Roanoke River had been taken by the Southern ironclad *Albermarle* armed with two 100-pounders. She was lying berthed at Plymouth. No normal-draft warship could approach the ironclad, so Cushing was given command of a steam launch with a spar torpedo, manned by a crew of thirteen.

Albermarle was protected by a 30-foot raft of floating logs, but the launch ran the gauntlet of opposing fire to push halfway into the log barrier. Meanwhile, one of the 100-pounders was being brought to maximum depression. Cushing's despatch reported: "My torpedo was exploded at the same time that the *Albermarle*'s gun was fired. A shot seemed to go crashing through my boat, and a dense mass of water rushed in from the torpedo, filling and completely disabling her; the enemy then continued to fire at fifteen feet range, and demanded our surrender, which I twice refused."

Three of the crew were taken, but Cushing leaped overboard and swam clear, while *Albermarle* sank at her moorings. Shortly afterward, the young lieutenant was appointed flag captain of the fleet.

9
Mechanized Menace

Though the sailing vessels of an earlier age were still common upon the high seas, the second half of the nineteenth century surrounded the seaman with technicians and their works. Iron and steam, armor and huge guns, tactics of a completely new order—it was another world. With this in view, the U.S. Government made an unheard-of gesture. A twin-turret monitor, *Miantonoma*, was sent out in 1867 on a world tour, to show the flag and an up-to-date warship. There was some doubt about the vessel's fitness for such a voyage, as she had less than three feet of freeboard, but she survived.

Miantonoma had two Parrott 480-pounder muzzle-loading smoothbores in each turret. These guns recoiled on a quadrant railtrack, which absorbed the energy and brought the muzzles at right angles to the gunport for reloading. Overhead runways, slings and hoists had to be used in the process; this was another feature of the changing times—the use of projectiles far beyond man-handling weight. An anonymous Royal Navy officer provided an account of gun-service as he saw it in one of *Miantonoma*'s turrets, during salute firing. He described the interior as about twelve feet in diameter, padded from top to bottom and dimly lamp-lit.

"Prepare!" was the first command ... "The gunner's mates stand you on your toes, and tell you to lean forward and thrust your tongue out of your mouth. You hear the creaking of machinery. It is a moment of intense suspense.
118

Gradually a glimmer of light—an inch—a flood. The shield passes from the opening—the gun runs out. A flash, a roar—a mad reeling of the senses, and crimson clouds before your eyes—a horrible pain in your ears...you find yourself plump up in a heap against the padding...They tell you that the best part of the sound has escaped through the

H.M.S. 'CAPTAIN'
1870

U.S.N. MONITOR 'MIANTONOMA', 1867.

port-hole, otherwise there would be no standing it, and our gunner's mate whispers in your ear: 'It's all werry well, but they busts out bleeding from the chest and ears after the fourth discharge, and has to be taken below.' "

Below decks was scarcely a suitable place for recovery. Our observer commented that the men's quarters were eight feet below the waterline, with upgoing pipes that did not succeed

119

in ventilating the area. During rough weather the seamen were confined in that incredibly foul atmosphere, much like the crew of a submarine. In fact, the latter were in better conditions, for they were few in number.

Americans had made the first practical use of submarines; France took the lead from the technical point of view. Charles Brun's *Plongeur* of 1863 was not only the biggest undersea craft to that date—it was the most powerful as well. It was 146 feet long by 12 feet diameter, with a compressed-air engine of 80 h.p. In spite of reasonable success on trials, the submarine gained no official support; the Emperor Napoleon III was more interested in ironclads.

French naval service at the time was organized on a pattern of national records, which originated in the time of Louis XIV (1643–1715). A boy destined for sea service was inscribed or listed, and until he reached 16 years he was classed as a *mousse* (shipboy), after a probationary year. At 16 he was rated apprentice (if he had been trained in a naval school) and at 18 he attained seaman status. He was then liable for service until he was 50 years old. There were five main naval stations—Cherbourg, Brest, Lorient, Rochefort, and Toulon. These were the focal points of the divisions; Brest and Toulon were first-class divisions, the others being second class. At each station, and all other main points, a Commissary-General and staff dealt with maritime inscription. Responsibility for manpower, supplies, and navigational matters rested with the Minister of Marine.

Inscription for naval service was applicable to all men whose livelihood depended on the sea, including shore workers. Any such man who had 1½ to 2 years' sea experience by the time he was 18 became liable, and at 20 he had to report to his local Commissary for service. After enrollment, he was sent to a main seaport to enter a division of seamen of the fleet. For an inscribed man, the term of service with the fleet was seven years from the age of 20. If he forestalled his call-up by joining at 18, there were some privileges. Renewable furlough (leave) without pay permitted him to work at coastal navigation.

Men who volunteered without inscription served only five years. Where a shortage of men caused a national call-up, each area held a draw with reference to a recruiting list. The men who drew the lowest numbers were recruited. Shore training arrangements provided an administrative council for each division, to deal with such items as clothing and pay. In the first-class divisions, the *matelot* (seaman) was in one of several groups—gunners, fusiliers, mechanics and stokers, inscribed seamen, or general recruitment personnel. Elementary schools, gymnasia, and swimming schools were included in the instructional department of the divisions. Marine infantry were trained, but they did not serve aboard except in wartime; their normal duties were in garrison.

Until the union of the German states under Prussia in 1871, the Prussian navy comprised only 55 ships of small size, led by two frigates. Under the Prussian Emperor, a nation-wide call-up was organized, so that men who preferred sea service to the army could have their choice. As in the French system, all fit men were called up at 18 (with a few exceptions) and service continued in some respect up to 42. Twelve years had to be served with the fleet, and the remaining time with the *Seewehr* (reserve). In emergency, any able man, even if not normally liable, could be called for service.

Russian naval recruitment followed the same general lines. All classes of males, without distinction, were liable for some form of military service, but the call-up was carried out by drawing lots to make up a number fixed annually. Those men who were 20 by January 1, came within the law, but recruits of a set educational standard were permitted to volunteer rather than to risk the lot with its directed service.

In the Royal Navy, as on the Continent, a number of

121

traditional seamen's duties were being gradually squeezed out as the machine encroached. It was no longer important to be nimble in the tops, to scramble with catlike agility aloft and down again. Instead, the clanking, oily engine room, the artificers, the stokers and coal trimmers were vital to the ship's well-being. Other personnel comprised three classes of seaman (leading, able, ordinary), Marines, and boys. From the ranks of the latter came seamen and petty officers, so able and ordinary seamen were rarely admitted direct into the Royal Navy. At the age of 18 a boy was entered for a period of ten years, subject to standard requirements in mental and bodily fitness.

A system of impressment was still being employed at the time of the Crimean War, though the Fleet was manned on that occasion without the press. British seamen who served foreign powers were recalled from that service in time of war, and warship commanders were directed to search foreign vessels for such men. Another ancient usage was the payment of prize money. This was awarded in ten classes, when officers down to the rank of captain had taken their shares. First class administrative officers, such as inspectors of steam machinery, had 45 shares of the remainder, while able seamen had four shares. These survivals seem to accord ill with the grim black-painted ironclads of the post-Crimean period, with airless candle-lit 'tweendecks and unfamiliar heat under a tropic sun. In the old wooden walls, the big square gunports could be opened for ventilation on the lower decks, but the turret ironclad had no ports. Even the small scuttles serving the officers' cabins were rarely unplugged.

After the establishment of the continuous ten-year service period, in 1853, shipboard routine became adapted to the new era. Shore leave was regularly given, both in home and foreign ports, and there was a general improvement in crew accommodation. Only gunboats remained cramped, through the space taken up by engines, boilers, and bunkers. One

122

particular rule applicable to wooden ships was still observed in those made of iron—no smoking was permitted below. Ratings could smoke on deck forward of the mainmast, and officers abaft the mast.

An age of mechanization had brought a changed relationship between officers and crew, so that discipline was maintained on a different basis. "Starters" were no longer in evidence, neither was the boatswain free with his cane as in former days. Though flogging was still in regulations, by the late 1860 decade it was almost entirely abolished in practice. Cleaning the *heads*, terms of imprisonment, or dismissal from the service, were the usual penalties. These were most commonly incurred for drunkenness, the age-old misdemeanor of the seaman. Through such concessions to humanity, the Navy regained the popularity lost during the 1850s, and the British seaman was once again the symbol of national pride.

Service on board still had problems peculiar to the age. Coaling was part of the routine; the coal was hoisted out of barges several bags at a time, by means of a whip rove to the yard. Stokers wheeled the bags away in iron trucks, to empty the coal down chutes leading to the bunkers. It was a filthy business. Coal dust lay thick everywhere, the seamen were black, and many hours of labor were required to restore all to order again.

Another aspect of naval life at that time was the battle of the designers. Unrigged ironclads of the 1860 decade showed the way to a clean, untrammeled design, but the Admiralty was still heavily biased toward auxiliary sail power. There was some reason for this. Many steam warships still lacked range through inadequate bunkers. Even in 1868 the round voyage to Gibraltar was not lightly undertaken. Designers were forced at last into making better bunker provision through the bad sailing qualities of iron armored vessels. However, while the controversy raged, the hapless seaman who had to

123

work the ships was ground between the upper and nether millstones.

Captain Phipps Cowper Coles, the British turret ship enthusiast, was prominent in the debate. After supervising the cut-down of *Royal Sovereign*, 121, to a turret ship (1862–64), Coles and Edward J. Reed co-operated in building *Monarch*. She was a rigged and armored twin-turret craft, launched in 1868, and on trials her 8,000 h.p. engines gave 15 knots.

Coles was not satisfied with *Monarch*, so he produced in 1869 an unusual vessel in *Captain*, 6,950 tons, 14 knots, with armor up to 13 inches, and six 25-ton 12-inch guns in twin turrets. She was a rigged ship, with the first tubular tripod masts. These were employed to dispense with shrouds; the designer wished to leave the field of fire clear for his turret guns. *Captain*'s extensive sail area and high masts gave excessive topweight—she was the only British warship to set maintopmast studding sails. This defect in weight disposal was combined with a light hurricane deck as superstructure, and a low freeboard. It appears that the original intention was a freeboard of 8 feet 6 inches, but by mistake the figure became reversed.

After two satisfactory cruises, *Captain* was caught in heavy weather off Cape Finisterre in the Bay of Biscay, on the night of September 6, 1870. Steam was up, but her engines were not in use, and her structural faults caused her to capsize. Only the gunner and 17 ratings survived, out of a complement of 490 officers and men. In a launch from the hurricane deck, the gunner steered his little party over mountainous seas to the Spanish shore. Captain Coles himself had been aboard his ill-fated ship as a passenger, and he went down with her.

A shock like this settled the design question, and from then on rigged warships were not favored. Increased bunker space and established coaling stations dealt with the fuel problem, and by 1871 the first seagoing unrigged ironclads were in commission in the Royal Navy. Edward Reed's *Devastation*, laid down in 1869, was a good example. She was 285 feet long by 62¼ feet beam, displacing 9,060 tons, and her two turrets, armored up to 14 inches, were enclosed in a redoubt of maximum 12 inches armor. Though *Devastation* had only 4 feet 6 inches of freeboard, she gained the most favorable reports as regards stability.

Encouraged by success, the Admiralty ventured still further into the unusual. H.M.S. *Inflexible*, on service in 1876, was a kind of pace setter; her main dimensions were 320 feet by 75 feet, her displacement was 11,880 tons, and her speed 12.8 knots. She mounted two turrets in echelon (diagonally across her breadth), so that her four 80-ton 12-inch guns had an extensive field of fire forward and aft. A total weight of 3,155 tons of armor protected the ship, with side armor 24 inches thick. *Inflexible*'s turret guns showed the technical advance of the times in that muzzle-loading was performed and the recoil absorbed by hydraulic means.

In loading, the muzzle was depressed to align with the loading hatch below decks, where a rammer was housed. A vertical hoist raised the encased charge of powder to the muzzle, for the hydraulic rammer to thrust it in; the shell was then hoisted, and the two items were rammed home together. As the gun was elevated to the firing position, rollers under the turret turned the latter as required. Sighting was done from a roof hatch, and the gun was fired by a friction tube and lanyard, or electrically by remote control. When the charge exploded, pistons attached to the trunnion housing conveyed the recoil to large horizontal hydraulic cylinders at the rear of the mounting.

This was a tremendous advance on the old nonrecoil mounting of 20 years before. It illustrates clearly that the seamen gunners in charge of such a system were necessarily of very different outlook from those who served the old ship artillery. This branch of naval service had its increasing number of sea technicians, just as other shipboard features were adding to the complexity of the floating fortress.

While this expansion was taking place, the most skilful and daring activities of the seaman were being given further opportunity. It was hatred of England that first spurred John

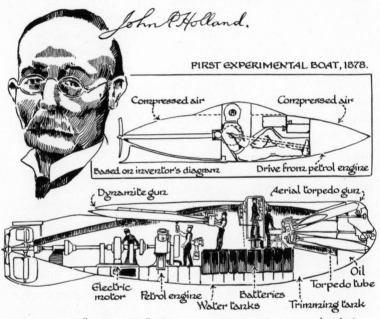

John P. Holland.

FIRST EXPERIMENTAL BOAT, 1878.

Compressed air   Compressed air

Based on inventor's diagram   Drive from petrol engine

Dynamite gun   Aerial torpedo gun

Oil
Torpedo tube
Electric   Petrol engine   Batteries   Trimming tank
motor   Water tanks

SUBMARINE "HOLLAND", 1898   Based on contemporary drawing.

Philip Holland (1842–1914) to devote himself to submarine design. He was born at Liscannor, Co. Clare, Ireland, and his burning patriotism desired to strike at England. After a good deal of work on plans, Holland emigrated to America in 1875, hoping to make enough money by teaching to finance his venture. This hope was not realized, but in 1877 funds from Sinn Fein, the Irish patriotic society, provided the

126

means to gain Holland's end.

Two fellow Irishmen named Todd and Rafferty made the inventor's experimental steel submarine, in their workshops at Paterson, New Jersey. It was tried on the Passaic River in May and June, 1878; the drawings for it show a cigar-shaped vessel about twelve feet long, with more than half its volume taken up by air supply compartments. Holland recorded the overall weight as 25½ hundredweight when the operator was aboard; this included nearly half a ton of lead ballast, as a safety weight, and about 3 hundredweight of water ballast. A number of typical Holland features were in this prototype. It dived by the admission of water, while horizontal planes controlled the depth of dive, and maintained the depth as long as there was forward speed. An important provision was that the water-ballast tank was divided into several sections, to prevent the water from surging to one end of the tank and upsetting the trim. If the engine stopped, the fact that the submarine's weight was less than its total buoyancy caused the reserve lift to bring it to the surface. In Holland's drawings, the operator is shown in diving dress.

Some defects of the prototype included an unreliable Brayton petrol engine, lack of visibility, and the vagaries of the compass when enclosed within the steel hull. After further experiments, including the use of what was then called an "optical tube" (a primitive periscope), Holland sank his plunging boat and concentrated on a second effort. This was the *Fenian Ram* of 1880, built with funds from the society, and it performed well. At one time, the *Ram* was being demonstrated in almost daily dives off New York.

Shortly after this, in 1883, the Swedish machine-gun inventor Nordenfelt built a steam submarine in Stockholm. His craft was 64 feet by 9 feet, displacing 60 tons submerged, with a 100 h.p. engine, giving a surface speed of eight knots. Two large reservoirs were stored with steam for use when submerged. In order to dive, water ballast was admitted until

127

the small conning tower, representing one hundredweight of reserve buoyancy, was just awash. Beside the conning tower were two vertical screw propellers worked by a 6 h.p. engine, which took over at that stage to provide downhaul. A depth gauge closed the throttle of the auxiliary engine when the safety depth (about sixty feet) was reached, and trim was maintained with bow rudders worked by a plumb weight.

Each of the two inventors decried the other's system. Nordenfelt declared that the steering-under principle risked crushing the bow through lack of depth control, while Holland criticized the downhaul device in that it could be ineffective through mechanical failure. When the U.S. Government invited designs for a submarine, in 1887, the rivals submitted their respective plans, and Holland's were accepted in 1893. His *Plunger*, launched in 1897, was 85 feet by 11½ feet, with a loaded displacement of 168 tons, and powered by triple-expansion steam engines. These were arranged to charge batteries as well as to drive the triple screws; the batteries served electric motors for submerged travel. Originally *Plunger* had an upright retractable exhaust duct, but when she was converted to petrol, in 1902, that was removed. Observation in both Holland and Nordenfelt submarines depended on the conning tower maintained awash, and *Plunger*'s four-foot tower was armored with four-inch steel.

When the latter was being built, the U.S. Government insisted on having downhaul screws as well as diving planes. Owing to disagreements over this, the vessel was never commissioned, and the inventor returned the Government advance. Meanwhile, he had been working on a little 53-foot submarine which he called *Holland*. It was launched at Lewis Nixon's Crescent Shipyard, in Elizabethport, New Jersey, on May 17, 1897. This small craft was to be the nucleus of the world's submarine fleets. She ran on a 45 h.p., 8-knot Otto petrol engine, with a 5½-knot dynamotor capable of 150 h.p.

for underwater cruising. These power plants gave ranges of 1,000 miles and 60 miles respectively.

Holland was armed with two 8.675-inch dynamite guns and one forward tube for a Whitehead locomotive torpedo. These weapons had been developed during the previous 30 years. Captain E.L. Zalinsky, U.S. Artillery, had produced the gun in 1888, on the lines of Mefford's pneumatic gun of 1883. It was really a great airgun, working at pressures up to 2,000 pounds p.s.i.; the submarine's Zalinsky gun fired a light steel shell to 6,000 yards. Dynamite was used in the original shells, hence the term dynamite gun, but blasting gelatine was adopted later. *Holland* was the first submarine to mount a gun of any kind.

Whitehead's torpedo was first produced in 1864. It combined the self-propelled, unmanned surface vessel proposed by Captain Luppis, of the Austrian navy, and the underwater improvements of the English engineer, Robert Whitehead, of Fiume.

In the 1864 torpedo, weighing 300 pounds, a compressed-air engine gave six knots and a quarter-mile range, while carrying 18 pounds of dynamite. Size and performance were increased so that within 15 years the missile measured 19 feet by 15 inches, travelling 15 feet under water at 24 knots to a 600-yard range. A hundred pounds of guncotton in the *warhead* depended for detonation on a steel percussion spike, called the *pistol*, screwed into the nose. Direction was maintained by a pendulum weight linked to a hydrostatic valve to check trim and depth, while together they reacted on the rudders. This weapon's contrarotating screws, which prevented rolling, were driven by a three-cylinder 40 h.p. engine running on air at 1,000 pounds p.s.i. All Holland's armed submarines had a compensatory arrangement, so that when loss of weight occurred, such as the firing of a torpedo, water ballast was taken in to compensate against loss of trim.

After exhaustive tests, *Holland* was accepted for the U.S.

129

Navy in April, 1900. An unexpected feature of the tests was the arrival of *Holland*, unmanned, at the Goldsmith and Tuthill basin, New Suffolk, on October 11, 1899. Everyone on board, passengers and crew, had been overcome by exhaust fumes.

10

Contest for Sea Power

While the Irish-American inventor was thrusting his way to success, the French, who had pioneered power submarines, were making great progress. An electric craft was completed in 1881 by Goubet of Paris, and it created such a good impression that several such vessels were ordered for the Imperial Russian Navy. In Goubet's submarine were included some useful ideas. He overcame the compass difficulty by using a one-piece cast bronze hull, surmounted by a seven-light conning tower. Trim was maintained by a clutch-controlled shaft which engaged pump gear to transfer water from one end tank to another, as required.

There was no vertical rudder; the screw was on a universal joint, so that its angle of thrust could be varied. One officer and a rating manned the vessel, sitting back to back with their heads in the conning tower, while the rating steered. Goubet's attack system was an old-type spiked torpedo mine, set outside the hull. When released, it rose in the water to fix its spikes under the objective, and the submarine retreated, to explode the charge through a connecting wire. This was a drawback, and another was that she carried no means of recharging her batteries. Later models by Goubet had compensating gear to regulate the depth by the intake or output of water, but none of the vessels seems to have exceeded six knots.

Several other French submarines were produced on electric propulsion. *Gymnote*, built at Toulon in 1888, was made of steel, 59 feet long and displacing 30 tons. She was notable in having a *gyrostat* to maintain direction—a wheel rotating on an invariable axis, which indicated any deflection from course. Two larger vessels of the same kind were *Gustave Zede* and *Morse*, each of 148 feet by 145 tons displacement. Both had bronze hulls, but lacked recharging gear. In 1897 Laubeuf designed *Narwal*, a steam submarine of 112 feet and 200 tons. She was built at Cherbourg in 1898, with triple-expansion engines and fuel-fired boilers, which plant charged the batteries for underwater use. On the surface the vessel made 11 knots, and 8 below.

Narwal had a unique form of hull for that time, with inner and outer casings for extra protection under attack, and the armored dome carried a short telescopic funnel. A pair of diving planes at each extremity prevented too steep an inclination when submerging. That operation originally took her 25 minutes, but training later halved the time.

In spite of careful compass reading, it was not easy to steer truly below, so French technicians had been at work on an *optical tube*. This had a total reflection prism at its upper extremity and another at the lower position, giving the commander a limited view of his surroundings. Philip Watts, F.R.S., Director of Naval Construction, Great Britain, wrote in 1901:

"Another instrument, the periscope, has received much attention. In this an image is formed in the focus of a parabolic reflector, and can then be examined by means of an ingenious optical contrivance; but this instrument has scarcely given all the results expected of it." Nevertheless, the French favored the periscope, and *Morse* was fitted with one in 1898.

By 1901, France had nine more electric submarines building, with plans for a fleet of 22 on the same lines. Batteries were housed amidships, with the motors astern of them, and the torpedo compartment was in the bows. In the lower part of the hull lay the ballast tanks, served by electric pumps, and below all the detachable lead ballast keel. In most cases, this type of vessel was manned by one officer and twelve ratings, who could remain submerged for at least 16 hours, with a safety depth of 75 feet.

There may have been an underlying reason for the French devotion to submarines. Rivalry was still strong between the two former enemies, so probably the incentive was to match the powerful British surface fleet.

Until 1901, the Admiralty merely observed the new trend. Then, despite the unsatisfactory features of the submarine, it was thought advisable to venture. Messrs. Vickers, Son, & Maxim, of Barrow, built the first British submarines—five of Holland's design, $63\frac{1}{3}$ feet by 11¾ feet, and of 120 tons. This class was powered by a 190 h.p. petrol engine, giving twelve knots from a 400-mile petrol tank. When submerged, the Vickers craft ran on a 70 h.p. electric motor that gave seven knots for four hours. A single bow tube was provided, and five torpedoes were housed forward. As the submarines were relatively small, they could be carried on the deck of a battleship and lowered into the water when they were needed.

Amid the crowding scientific and technical devices of the age, it was very clear that the seaman was becoming dwarfed. In the days of sail, a ship's life was her crew, swarming in the rigging to deal with canvas, clustered upon the gundecks in action, about the hundred tasks of maintenance found in a wooden ship. Yet a single cruiser of 1900, with her steel armor, her high-speed mechanical propulsion, and her vastly superior firepower, could have destroyed the whole of Nelson's fleet without ever coming within range of the smoothbore muzzle-loaders. Though a few of the intermediate type of massive turret muzzle-loaders survived in the Navy until 1902, breechloaders were almost universal at that time. In action, the up-to-date warship appeared as if devoid

133

of human life, a mere closed-up automaton steaming onward and firing.

That aspect, more than any other, displayed the enormous advances of the nineteenth century. From the first clumsy ironclads of the Crimean War, little more than 40 years had encased the fighting seamen in armor as a matter of course. A most curious feature of seafaring life was that, as technology increased its scope, a lesser proportion of seamen were able to swim. Possibly this was due to the increased feeling of security in an iron, armored ship.

One of the contributions to the new order of British seamen had been the Education Acts from 1870 onward. When compulsory schooling finally became widespread, it provided mental training that could grapple with the complexities of life on a mechanized ship. However bright or dull the product of the elementary school, the discipline and the habit of learning resulted in a more receptive mind than would have been possible in earlier days.

It was especially valuable in the submarine service, that perilous undertaking for volunteers. Even on the surface, the atmosphere below was thick and stuffy; when closed up for diving it became oppressive. Usually, the watch below was instructed to lie down, so that they consumed less air than if they had been moving about. Engine vibration seemed more intense, filling the ears and dulling the senses; the knowledge that an immense weight of water was exerting fearful pressure upon the steel shell—the hushed voices, the downcast eyes, in an atmosphere of unreality. In that clammy house of steel, the sweat ran down the pale faces, and clothes hung wetly. No man dared think of the possibilities—engine failure, unreliable instruments, through which a vessel might dive too deeply and be crushed.

In spite of known and unknown perils, the eternal resilience of the seaman adapted his manner of life to meet the difficulties below. One of the first divisions from surface life was the decline of shaving, a nuisance under submarine conditions, so the below-surface seaman grew a beard. Common perils shared tended to relax the rigidity of rank discipline—officers and seamen became a co-operative rather than a directed unit. Further concessions were made as regards rig, which permitted free and easy attire on sea service.

An early twentieth century submarine was a surface vessel that was able to dive for attack or to escape. It was not designed for extensive underwater cruises, like those of the present day. However, deep diving was an essential part of training, and by 1905 the limit was 100 feet. Submarine exercises had seen some perils and tragedies by that date. Two of the improved A-class units, A1 and A8, had been lost, in one case through collision, and in the other, a dive with the conning tower open, off Plymouth Sound. Several instances of diving plane failure had been recorded, and one of strained plates causing leaks.

A strange mishap befell A4 at Portsmouth in October, 1905. She was taking part in tests connected with the hydrophone underwater listening device. During the tests, A4 was just below the surface, with a four-inch brass ventilator tube protruding above. Through this a flag was used to signal sound reception. Suddenly A4 sank out of control, reaching 90 feet; gallons of seawater were flooding her, and despite efforts to blow the tanks, intake was faster than output.

It was a severe test of discipline. A4 lurched down by the bows at 40 degrees, and the lights went out; her crew were trapped in blackness, with water pouring into their steel coffin. Leading Seaman Baker, a hydroplane coxswain, located the inrush at the brass ventilator and tried to screw in the cap, but the force was too great. Having tried to stuff the opening with seamen's caps, Baker dragged off his jersey, and succeeded in stopping the flow with that. Even then, there was deadly danger. Floods of water were swishing about

135

inside the hull, and some had reached the batteries, producing chlorine gas.

Providence decreed that, with the inflow checked, the tanks could be blown effectively, and A4 wallowed to the surface, stern first. All hands were ordered on deck, but on calling the roll, the captain, Lieutenant Martin Nasmith (later Second Sea Lord) found that two men were missing. Plunging again into the darkness and the chlorine fumes, he found the two at their stations—they had not heard the captain's order. H.M.S. *Hazard* then took the submarine in tow, but before she could be brought into dock, three internal explosions took place, and A4 settled on the bottom. On inquiry, it was found that the wash from a passing steamer had flooded the submarine's ventilator, and thus imperilled the entire crew.

Britain's venture into submarines had much amused the German authorities, whose navy was relatively new. The first naval program of the German Empire had been presented in 1872. When the Kaiser Wilhelm II (1859—1941) succeeded his father in 1888, he devoted his attention to the building of a powerful navy that would balance his land forces. Public reaction was unfavorable—German manpower was already under conscription. Nevertheless, when the Kaiser was invited to the Royal Navy review at Spithead, in 1889, the royal yacht, *Hohenzollern*, was escorted by seven battleships and four light craft.

An impressive British array was drawn up at Spithead—20 battleships, 29 cruisers, and over 60 other vessels. It was a splendid show, but the shrewd eye of the Kaiser noted that the Royal Navy was not really organized for war. This was the opinion of Admiral Sir Edmund Fremantle, as expressed in his reminiscences of that period: "We had large crews, and, as all the ships were masted, there was a fair amount of sail drill, while I fear gunnery was little attended to."

At the time of the review, the Channel Fleet of five ships was the only fully commissioned force in home waters; the

British center of patrol activity was the Mediterranean. There was much the same position in the French navy, while Russia ruled alone in northern waters. Accordingly, the German fleet training was done in the Baltic. With that force, as with the other great navies of the world, the Royal Navy was its pattern as regards structure. When Alfred von Tirpitz (1849—1930), son of a judge, became Secretary of the Imperial Navy in 1897, a new era began. Von Tirpitz specialized in torpedoes very early in his career.

From 1898, the Secretary was driving for a great naval program. His Bill of 1900 required a new fleet, with 32 battleships; in a footnote he declared: "At the moment we are almost helpless against England at sea."

Armor and armament were the prime targets. Steel had first been used on British warships in 1875, but it was brittle compared with wrought iron. Various toughening systems had overcome the problem, chiefly the American Harvey process, which carbonized the face of armor plate. Best of all was the nickel steel produced by Krupp of Essen, in Westphalia, Prussia, a large concern founded by Friedrich Krupp in 1810. During trials in 1895 an 11.8-inch Krupp plate resisted three 12-inch projectiles, so Britain and America adopted that form of armor in 1896. Krupp steel tubes were employed for the inner lining of Germany's guns, giving a life of up to 220 rounds before renewal, while British wire-wound guns were only good for 60 rounds. A great defect of the Krupp gun was the sliding lateral breechblock, which was drawn out to the left for loading; it left a clear run for the shell like the old Armstrong. This block was liable to damage in action. It was inferior to the French system used by Britain—a hinged block with a sleeve carrying an interrupted thread. One-eighth of a turn locked and sealed the breech.

There was a vast difference between the respective systems of the Royal Navy and the Imperial German Navy. In the

137

former, service was voluntary, with a short active period, followed by transfer to the reserve. German seamen nearly all served 12 years, and they had to re-enlist for another ten years to get a pension. As with the British system, compulsory education had created a more intelligent type of recruit. A limited number of men and boys served for five

SEAMAN, U.S. NAVY, 1898.

years, with seven in the *Seewehr*. Cadets entered the Imperial Navy at 16, for brief shore training, then, after a spell in a Training Squadron ship they went to sea. Some entries at 17½ went right away to the training ship. This differed greatly from the British practice, by which cadets of 13½ went to Naval Colleges for four years before going on training ships.

138

The German authorities considered that three years' sea training produced a seaman. Every year a third of the conscripts passed into the reserve, equalling in the number the new intake, and the winter months were spent breaking in the new cadets. Between October and May, fighting ships did duty as training centers. Volunteers who re-enlisted formed the backbone of the navy, and from these the petty officers were chosen.

It was a notable feature of all naval training by 1900 that seamanship was not a basic requirement—there was so much technical work and maintenance that a large part of the crew dealt with this. Still, naval traditions such as tenacity of purpose and split-second reaction to command were even more important in the great complex fighting machine. There had never been such constant endeavor at high pressure in any navy. Only the best was good enough; officers gained promotion direct from the Kaiser, who was merciless upon slackness. He was an active commander-in-chief, with personal control and his orders were concise without details; the subordinate had to use his wits. Under this regime, class distinction was completely rigid; there was no promotion out of the social class. If lower-grade engineers aspired to the officer class, they were forbidden to marry, and they had to serve two years in foundries and engineering workshops.

An unspoken rivalry between British and German naval authorities led to a continual struggle for supremacy in building. In 1906, Britain took the lead with *Dreadnought*, 18,000 tons, 500 feet by 82 feet. She was a revolutionary warship, with no secondary armament, as well as being the first capital ship to use the steam turbine. This motive power was first applied to a ship by (Sir) Charles Parsons (1854–1931), and it was demonstrated unofficially at the Spithead Review in 1897. Basically the turbine consists of a rotor with thousands of tiny blades on closely packed discs along its length. It is mounted on a shaft, with end bearings, in a casing with corresponding fixed blades inside it. Steam entering the casing at one end impinges upon the blades of the rotor to spin it at high speed. In the new warship, the turbines were of 23,000 h.p., producing 21 knots.

Dreadnought mounted two 12-inch guns forward on her centerline, high above the deck, and on each side at high level

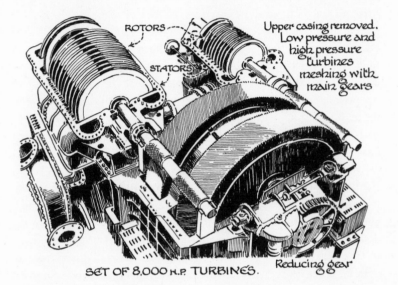

SET OF 8,000 H.P. TURBINES.

was another pair of 12-inch guns. This gave six guns for ahead fire, or four on either broadside. Two pairs of 12-inch were mounted aft, one pair astern of the other, and there five low-level torpedo tubes (some vessels fired from deck tubes). Though the gun weight was raised high, it was balanced by the turbines, which were set lower in the hull than ordinary engines. Such a heavyweight warship was a blow to the *Reichsmarineamt*, though a German move of the same year was immensely significant. *Unterseeboot 1* (U-1) was commissioned at Kiel in 1906, the first of the U-boats whose name was to spell terror. U-1 displaced 240 tons on the surface, with eleven knots, and nine submerged.

In addition to capital ships, two small types had received much attention from all naval powers during the previous years. Early in 1872, Messrs. Thorneycroft had built *Miranda*, a 45-foot, 16½-knot *torpedo-boat*, the first of its kind. It was designed to high-speed attack with its single torpedo-tube. Four years later the Royal Navy received its first torpedo-boat, *Lightning*, 19 knots. Speed, size, and hitting power were increased, until by 1885 such boats did 21½ knots, with three tubes and six 3-pounders.

One of the first ships especially designed to combat the menace was the French *Bombe,* of 1885. She carried heavier weapons than the torpedo boats, and on this type was based the *torpedo boat destroyer*, such as the Royal Navy's *Daring* of 1892. This vessel was 185 feet long, doing 27 knots, with a 12-pounder, three 6-pounder quick-firing guns, and three tubes. Quick-firing guns had electric batteries which fired the shell as soon as the breech was closed.

It was soon decided that the new vessels could be applied to the functions of a torpedo boat as well as to its own protective purpose, so the smaller type declined. When the turbine was used in *destroyers*, as they were later called, H.M.S.*Cobra* of 1899 was the earliest turbine warship, with a speed of over 34 knots.

This European contest was of interest to American authorities, for their country had suffered its usual postwar decline, through public dislike of peace-time forces. After the Civil War, many green-timber cruisers rotted, and during twenty years both warships and merchantmen were of poor quality. Nearly 80 per cent of U.S. Navy seamen were aliens, and the Navy fell from second place to twelfth. It was the upheaval in Chile, in 1891, that brought a revival of American naval strength through incidents between the two countries' ships and nationals.

Congress permitted the building of coast defense

141

battleships drawing 24 feet of water, for use in rivers and inlets. They were protected by armor up to 20 inches, and armed with 13-inch and 8-inch guns. Normally U.S. warships were painted white, but two reports of the Spanish-American War mention the use of lead-colored paint. Cuba, at that time (1898) still a Spanish colony, was the cause of the war. Spanish harshness in Cuba had been observed with

H.M.S. HANNIBAL, 1897 (MAJESTIC CLASS).
First British class with Harvey steel armour.

disapproval by the Americans, among whom there was sympathy for rebels against the regime.

War would probably have broken out as early as 1873, had America then possessed a navy. In November of that year, 53 of the crew of *Virginius*, an American trading vessel, were shot by a Spanish firing squad in Santiago for running horses and supplies to the rebels. Over a hundred of *Virginius*'s crew were saved by Sir Lambton Loraine, in the Royal Navy sloop *Niobe*. He cleared for action and threatened to destroy the shipping in the anchorage if the shooting continued. This had

142

the desired effect: the Spanish agreed to pay indemnity, return the ship and salute the U.S. flag. Actually, the flag was hoisted in an obscure port, with no spectators, and *Virginius*, crippled by sabotage, sank on her way home.

During the course of the Cuban revolt which began in 1895, the U.S. Government sent *Maine* to take off American nationals, but she was sunk by mysterious explosions in the anchorage at Havana (February 1898). Only two of her fifteen boats were available for service; she lost 260 seamen in all—the greatest U.S. naval disaster to that date. War was declared by Congress on April 25, and Commodore George Dewey, then aged 61, was in charge of naval operations.

Manila Bay was the scene of the major sea action, where powerful forts supported the main Spanish fleet. A number of gunnery defects became apparent in the American warships. On *Olympia*, the flagship, many shells became detached from their cases in loading, so that they had to be rammed out from the muzzle end. Time after time shells jammed in loading, or the cases stuck in the breech after firing, and *Baltimore*'s electric firing gear was so bad that the gunners were forced back on the percussion tube system.

It was so hot in the turrets that the gun crews were kept outside it until the last moment and, in any lull, they were ordered out for fresh air. On the 8-inch rifled gun, the crew numbered eight—captain, plugman (who set the firing gear), loader, sponger, lifter and shellman. Shells for the 28-foot gun weighed 250 pounds, and they left the muzzle at 2,000 feet per second. There was a telescopic sight, and fire was directed from a conning tower on the roof of the turret. In spite of mechanical difficulties, the U.S. gunners destroyed the entire Spanish fleet between 5.15 a.m. and 1 p.m. on May 1, 1898. Eight wounded men were the only casualties on the attackers' side, and no ship was disabled. Early in July, a Spanish squadron was sunk off Santiago, which concluded the naval action in the war. At the end of November, Spain

143

ceded the Philippine Islands to America and withdrew from Cuba.

A repercussion of the gunnery troubles came early in the Presidency of Theodore Roosevelt (1858–1919), who was in office from 1901 to 1909. Captain (later Rear–Admiral) William Sims wrote direct to the President from the China Station, to the effect that U.S. ships had only registered five per cent hits during the Spanish War. Roosevelt knew of the Royal Navy gunnery expert Captain Percy Scott, whose director-firing system brought 80 per cent hits on the target. When U.S. naval units were tested, only 13 per cent hits were registered, so, by the President's order, Sims took charge of gunnery for a time.

Captain Scott's brilliance in gunnery became a byword. His cruiser, *Terrible*, was in effect a gunnery school, where he and his officers paid personal attention to gunners' training. By this means averages between 76 per cent and 92 per cent on target were achieved. Gun mounting was the captain's especial interest, and his ingenuity was of great value during the Boer War (1899–1901). *Terrible* arrived at Cape Town at the time when the Boers were threatening with encirclement the towns of Ladysmith, Mafeking and Kimberley. A call had come in from Ladysmith asking for a naval 4.7 to check the Boer artillery. British troops in the town had only field guns against long-range siege pieces.

Scott hoisted out two of *Terrible*'s 4.7s, and mounted them on cross bases, each formed by four 14-inch baulks of timber. These guns were sailed to Durban, from which they reached Ladysmith a short time before the besiegers closed in (November 2, 1899) for 119 days. A few days later, the gunnery expert was given charge of Durban's defenses, so he took with him 24 4.7s on mounts of his own design. This provided iron disc wheels and a double trail, so that the breech could pass down between the sides for the highest elevation.

In response to a special request, Scott mounted a 4.7 on a railtruck, providing a lift-off arrangement to allow the gun to be used from a platform. General Sir Redvers Buller asked for a six-inch ship gun on a mobile mounting, which Captain Scott designed. Later a light carriage for a 4.7 was needed, so the shipboard mount was removed, and the gun, in its recoil

NAVAL BRIGADE RATING, 1900.
Note good conduct stripes.

cradle, was set down on the axle. These various provisions were only made possible by Scott's ingenuity and the superlative skill of *Terrible*'s artificers, but the value of long-range naval guns in the field was incalculable.

Further contributions to the land action were made by the Naval Brigade. They were issued with khaki serge uniforms,

145

with turned-up soft felt hats, bearing the foul anchor badge for seamen and a bugle badge for Royal Marines. In the column heading for Ladysmith (relieved February 28, 1900), the Brigade gave the best example of gallantry under heavy fire. It was reported that the seamen coolly lowered their sights as the range shortened, instead of "aiming off" with the fixed sight at 500 yards, in the normal way. Army drill books decreed that men should not be allowed to lie during the last 500 yards of the advance, as they would not rise again to charge in the face of close-range magazine fire. This was disproved by the Brigade, who did just that, charging like dervishes upon the Boer rifles.

11
Titanic Combat

Early in the twentieth century, the western world was startled by news of a naval catastrophe. This was brought about by Japan, the one-time insular nation of the Far East. Japan had made such a rapid advance in military training that she was able to quarrel with China over the independence of Korea. During the resultant war (July 1894–March 1895) some idea of Japanese prowess was given. In mid-September, 1894, near the mouth of the Korean Yalu River, eleven Japanese cruisers, some armor-belted, of 4,000 tons, met a Chinese force. It comprised two 7,000-ton battleships, twelve cruisers, and six gunboats. After a brief clash, four Chinese vessels were sunk, and the rest were chased into port.

A futile move by the defeated force was the attempted use of the ram. This outdated appendage was a feature of most later nineteenth century warships, in the form of an outward underwater curve at the stem. As the Chinese found, gunpower in the 1890s made ramming a hopeless effort. Japan's naval strength and the standard of her army brought about a treaty of alliance with Great Britain in 1902.

Foreign observers saw in the Japanese Navy a model of efficiency. Their training school at Etajima used working models of battleship engines and of the six-inch Armstrong Elswick gun. Big gun drill was carried out in a long shed laid out like a gundeck, with a broadside battery of six-inch guns and a nine-inch bow gun. Trained gun crews could load and fire in eight seconds, though the six-inch shells weighed

100 pounds each. On board, Japanese seamen were never idle, and there was no punishment. Every man had obedience ingrained, and all were good-tempered. Ship routine was based on frequent drill and practice. Firing exercises were always at long range, and in action fire might be opened at 10,000 yards.

Big warships had two cooks, one Japanese and one foreigner, while the food was strictly inspected before and after cooking. Every day, the ship's doctor and the

IMPERIAL JAPANESE NAVY, 1905: SEAMEN & BATTLESHIP 'HATSUCE'.

quartermaster made a snap check, to see and taste the food. Daily rations for the lower deck comprised two small fish, pickles, a root vegetable called *okra*, which was thought to be very strengthening, and a plentiful supply of rice. All mess traps, consisting of iron plates and cups, knives, forks and spoons, were arranged on swinging shelves.

It has been remarked that the Royal Navy was the father of all the great navies of the world, by providing instructors and serving as a pattern. One feature was very widely adopted; the Japanese seaman, like many other nationals, wore the type of uniform first regularized in the Royal Navy in 1857. He had the frock or jumper, square turnover collar, bell-bottoms, and flat ribboned cap with the ship's name upon it. Fatigue dress consisted of a loose linen coat and trousers, with a wide-brimmed straw hat. In winter a long greatcoat, hooded and caped, a white muffler and wellington boots were on issue. Ratings washed their clothes under four large sampanlike boats resting on booms over the after hatch, and clotheslines were arranged there. Any repairs to uniforms were carried out by women workers in port.

It was this highly organized navy that clashed with the Russians in 1904, through rivalry over the development of Manchuria. At the time, Russia's navy was large, but it was fatally divided between the Far East, the Black Sea and the Baltic, with immense distances between. Seamen had only a shortened period of service, through climatic difficulties: the call-up was scheduled for 21-year-olds, while men of other navies had been years in training before that age. There was no instruction in naval tactics at the St. Petersburg school, though the naval intelligence service was supreme. Confidential material from every navy of note was on issue to Russian units.

In Manchuria, the key strategic base was Port Arthur, at the tip of the Kwantung Peninsula. At the time of the outbreak, the Russian Far Eastern Fleet had permission from China to winter there. Admiral Makarov was then the only capable Russian commander. His fleet at Port Arthur comprised 7 battleships, 11 cruisers, 25 destroyers, and a number of auxiliaries. A surprise torpedo attack in February, 1904, did considerable damage to the fleet, but Makarov skilfully regrouped his forces. Shortly afterward the Admiral was drowned in his mined flagship, and his successor, Admiral Vitgelft, died in action.

By August, the fleet was so badly damaged that repair in

the Port Arthur dockyard was impossible, so guns and seamen were landed to help the land defense. Several of the big ships were sunk at their moorings by Japanese attacks, or scuttled later when the fall of Port Arthur seemed near (surrender occurred in January 1905).

Meanwhile the Russian Baltic Fleet was laboriously making

RUSSIAN SEAMAN, 1905.

its way to the scene, a seven-months voyage around the Cape. This force of ageing units, seven battleships and six cruisers, was supported by a number of destroyers. While the fleet was traversing the North Sea, some Hull trawlers near Dogger Bank were reported as being Japanese torpedo boats, and fire was opened (October 21, 1904). One trawler was sunk, with the loss of two men. This error almost caused war with

Britain, but apologies and an indemnity settled the matter.

Command of the Japanese Navy was in the hands of Admiral Heihachiro Togo (1847–1934). On May 27, 1905, his smaller but superbly trained battle fleet met the ill-organized Russians at Tshushima, in the strait between Korea and Japan. It was a massacre. With their rapid and accurate gunfire, opened at long range, the Japanese destroyed or captured practically all the opposing force. Only one small cruiser, *Almaz*, and two destroyers reached port.

Two such shattering defeats added fuel to the smoldering fires of revolution among the Russian seamen. Conditions in the fleet had created widespread mutinous feelings by 1903. Rations and winter kit were the main grievances, both being scanty and of poor quality, while the crews' quarters were unbearably cramped and unventilated. Seamen were frequently forced to dock labor, and corruption among the officers led to victimization of those below them in status.

At last an issue of maggotty meat brought a violent outbreak aboard the Black Sea battleship *Potemkin*, in June, 1905. A number of officers and other ranks were shot dead, while in the port of Odessa a great demonstration was taking place. *Potemkin*'s mutinous crew took the ship to Odessa, where a conference of generals was being held in a theater. Attempts to bombard the theater with a six-inch gun resulted only in hits on the soldiers' barracks, which roused the animosity of the troops. Shortly afterward, the crew proclaimed freedom and security for all foreigners in the Black Sea.

When four other warships arrived at the port, they were required to surrender to *Potemkin*, on which the Red Flag was flying. One of the ships, *George the Victorious*, signalled that she allied herself with the mutineers, but later she deserted. Matters on board *Potemkin* were in some confusion; the ship was due for coaling, so the crew headed her southeast for the Crimean port of Feodosia. There they

151

were fired upon by soldiers in garrison, which dispirited them. After some debate, the ill-planned revolt came to an end when *Potemkin* sailed west again to the Rumanian port of Constanta, where she was surrendered.

Though the 1905 revolution was crushed, its embers remained to fire up again in the bloody destruction of 1917.

Over the rest of Europe, during the years of feverish arming and training that preceded 1914, the topic of maritime power was well to the fore. Big battleships still appeared as the prime factor, though the submarine had gained importance since the French brought out their diesel-engined craft, *Emeraude* and *Opale*, in 1906. Diesel power provided far greater reliability, increased range and simplified maintenance. Its operation depended on the high compression of fuel vapor in the cylinders, producing incandescence which made sparking plugs unnecessary. Other technical advances were the use of Marconi's wireless signalling apparatus, first mentioned as being in some warships in 1900, and the development of anti-submarine devices. By 1916, the hydrophone, for detecting the sound of engines under water was being developed.

Britain's immense surface power tended to bottle up the German High Seas Fleet, despite the very high standard of training in the latter. Again the familiar device of submarine warfare was employed by the weaker surface navy. Merchant ships were the major target; by extensive sinkings Britain's vital overseas supplies could be seriously checked. Though camouflage dazzle stripes were devised for ships by the great marine artist, Norman Wilkinson, the destruction went on.

During the first two years of war, traders sailed independently. Though convoys had been suggested, the merchant captains did not feel happy about mass movement, and the Royal Navy was too short of small warships for convoy duty. Lookout spells had a new significance—in addition to watching for other ships, the lookout had to observe the unnatural ripple of foam around the periscope of a U-boat, or the bubble track of a torpedo.

A hail from the masthead, at the same time as the dreaded black shape heaves itself out of the sea a few hundred yards away. Under the fixed gaze of the assembled crew, the conning–tower hatch opens. Across the intervening water

1914:
GERMAN RATING: SHORE DUTY RIG.

comes the megaphone message from a half-visible figure: "Abandon ship! I am going to sink you!"

Now the hurried bundling-up of gear, checking the boat stores, getting boats into water while the black thing hovers watching. Away, with the short sea stroke, the oarsmen staring fascinated, wordless, at the last act of the drama. They are too low upon the water to mark the track of

153

bubbles. There is no warning before the sudden bellowing crash, the pillared gust of smoke and the bursting column of white water. The ship is down by the head—she is heeling to port—gone, with the muffled thud of bursting boilers below. Gone, too, is the evil shape, and the wide sea is empty but for the toiling boats far from land.

It was accepted that the doomed ship should be warned, but with the increasing ferocity of the war it was not always so. Terror rode the winds and the dark as the lumbering convoys of early 1917, with their destroyer escort, crept onward to the distant goal. Food and munitions, fuel for the first war of the internal combustion engine, borne onward in metal shells exposed to the seawolf's attack. Far more deadly was the peril to the merchant seaman than to the naval rating; the latter at least was in a warship, and trained for war.

A hit—the night shattered and on fire with a blaze that is gone at once. In spite of patient drill, it is hard to keep from frantic rushing—there are screams below—the engine room is a hell of scalding steam, and they are trapped there. Such a lurch that all on deck are flung heaped against the starboard rail. It gives way, and the black water takes them, choking in the thick scum of oil that pours from her. Now the deep plunge, taking down with her the trapped and the dead, sucking into the whirlpool those who thrashed too close at her stricken side as they fought hopelessly for life.

Now and then, like some ghastly glimpse of another world, the glare flashes up anew with a further deathblow. Far across the field of broken light, the wreckage is tossing, heads among it, white upturned faces, clinging hands—all plunged again into the pit of dark, after a revealing instant. A bitter price for food.

In that ceaseless contest, hunting U-boat and fugitive tradeship, there was a third factor in the submarine killer. Destroyers were paramount here—light, fast, equipped with

GUN-HATCH CLOSED.

RAISING THE GUN.

GUN READY.

Based on official German photos.

WATERPROOF GUN-HOUSING FOR U-BOATS, 1914.

155

detector gear, depth charges and quick-firing guns. On rare
occasions unwary U-boats might be caught on the surface
and rammed, but most kills were the result of patient
hunting. It was the depth charge that took over then, that
simple oil drum form with its 300 pounds of high explosive.
A depth gauge was set so that the detonator mechanism (the
pistol) operated at the given pressure. These charges could be
rolled overboard or projected to about forty yards by a
special mortar. Usually a diamond pattern of charges was
thrown out over a suspected area to enclose it.

Fifty feet below, the strained white faces, bedewed with
sweat that gleams in the dim electric light; every man's eye
drawn upward as the harsh grinding of the hunter's engines
swells in approach, until it thunders overhead. Breathing
stops . . . the dreadful sound passes on. Silent still they hang,
suspended by the air trapped in the buoyancy tanks, until the
menacing beat has faded to nothing. Throughout the hull
now vibrates a throbbing tremor—it is safe to be running the
engines. Safe? As if from nowhere, on each quarter comes
grating in the roar of passing engines, and seconds later
everything is madness, and confusion of tangled arms and
legs. Amid deafening thunder the vessel rolls and pitches like
a paper boat in a mill race.

Scarcely could they rear up shakily from the welter when
again the depths were riven by the terrific shock waves.
Already great spouts of water were hissing a glittering pattern
across and across, in the light of the single remaining bulb.
She could not live; it was death for all of them did they not
surface. With blowers urging the water from her tanks, she
lurches upward, breaking into the open bow first. Low grey
shapes on each side; then a white sheet whipping in the wind
from the top of the conning tower, and the armed boats'
crews to bring off the prisoners. At least it is life for them,
and not a rat's death, shut in a steel tomb whose sides were
breaking in on them.

Despite the herculean efforts of the anti-submarine patrol,
the hidden enemy continued to score heavily, especially in

the Western Approaches off the south and west of Ireland. On these routes, supply ships from the Bay of Biscay and the Atlantic headed in to the main ports.

In October 1915, the Q-ship campaign had first begun. These battered, lumbering decoy traders were armed with concealed guns and manned by Royal Navy men in rough merchantmen's dress. This was a voluntary service, into which went serving and Reserve seamen, some with 20 years' experience at sea, others with a few months. Their captains needed first-class seamanship and unusual initiative. If a captain could lure an attacking U-boat within comfortable range, a single shot through her casing would prevent her from diving to escape.

Some nice play-acting was arranged on the decoy. If the ship was torpedoed, a frantic "Abandon ship" was muddled, boats lowered so clumsily as to spill the occupants, men throwing articles overboard and jumping after them. All the time steam was being blown off, and at last the disordered boats moved off, fumbling their rowing piteously. With a nonchalant air, the U-boat captain surfaced and circled his prey to choose the point for a final blow. During this interim, the hidden gun crews, in false deckhouses and similar cover, lay poised for action. At last the key moment—a certain shot. Down with the masking devices, swing out the guns and fire like madmen.

Q-ships normally carried timber cargoes to help flotation if they were severely damaged. This was frequently the case, for if the attacker escaped the element of mystery was lost. This is how the German authorities became aware of "trap ships," as they called them. Britain's leading Q-commander was Lieutenant (later Rear Admiral) Gordon Campbell, V.C., D.S.O. He took over the first "mystery ship," *Farnborough* (Q5), and gained the Victoria Cross in that perilous service.

After one of *Farnborough*'s successful missions (February 1917) she was in such danger, without hope of assistance, that Campbell radioed to the Admiralty: "Q5 slowly sinking respectfully wishes you goodbye." However, a destroyer picked up the signal, and brought the crippled ship into port. An instance of even more desperate action occurred in August, 1917, when Campbell was patrolling with his third Q-ship, the collier *Dunraven*, and his old crew. At a point

Q-SHIP'S HIDDEN GUN: DUMMY DECK LOCKER.

"Q-5 SLOWLY SINKING RESPECTFULLY WISHES YOU GOODBYE"
'Farnborough' after sinking U 83.

some 130 miles west of Ushant, in the mouth of the English Channel, they encountered UC 71, with the ace commander Saltzwedel. As the latter knew about trap ships, he opened fire at 5,000 yards, and kept up the fire as he approached.

Campbell maintained the "attacked merchantman" role, sending frantic appeals for help, and making ineffectual short shots with the little 2½-pounder that some cargo ships carried. He made clouds of steam, to suggest boiler damage, stopped engines, and sent away his "panic party" in boats. A great danger was the large supply of munitions on board; Lieutenant Bonner was blown right out of his control position when a shell exploded a depth charge in the poop. On crawling back, he found the poop on fire, but he and his group stayed there, scorched and choking, to maintain the deception. Some men held up cordite boxes from the hot deck. Soon after this, another explosion of depth charges and cordite blew the four-inch gun and its· crew all over the ship. Only one gun would bear, but the U-boat submerged to avoid its fire, and torpedoed *Dunraven* amidships.

There seemed to be no hope. In the last effort at bluff, Campbell sent away further boats and a raft. UC71 then surfaced astern, and shelled the ship at short range. Bonner and his wounded crew, disciplined to the last, were lying quiet amid the splinters of steel and exploding cordite boxes, the epitome of the British seaman. Previously Campbell had signalled off a warship which answered his mock call for help, but having fired his torpedoes without success, he decided to make a real call. Two British destroyers·and an American cruiser came to the rescue. *Dunraven* was taken in tow, but she finally sank by the stern. When making awards of decorations to the ship's company, King George V said, "Greater bravery than was shown by all officers and men on this occasion can scarcely be conceived."

By November, 1918 Britain had nearly three thousand small ships actually hunting U-boats, of which Germany had 170, with about fifty operating at once. By that date the total of U-boat killings had risen from two a month (April, 1917) to fourteen a month (May, 1918). This was the effect of the convoy system, largely owing to the persuasion of Admiral Sims, U.S.N., who went to England to co-operate with the Admiralty when America entered the war.

A great morale booster was the spectacular attack on the

U-boat base at Zeebrugge, on the Belgian coast nine miles from Bruges (April 23, 1918). Admiral Sir Roger Keyes, in *Warwick*, led a naval and Marine landing force which destroyed gun positions on the 1½-mile mole. Blockships were then sunk at the canal entry to prevent submarines from getting out. Though the channel was later cleared, the raid was most effective. *Vindictive* (Captain A.F.B. Carpenter) earned undying fame at Zeebrugge.

It was the little ships of the Allied fleets which saw most action. Only once did the massive floating fortresses of the Royal Navy see a large-scale engagement. At the Battle of Jutland, May 31–June 1, 1916, for the first and last time, two armored fleets were present in full force for battle. Britain's Admiral Jellicoe commanded 151 warships of all classes, from battleships to destroyers, and the German Admiral Scheer had 112.

Scheer had intended to make a demonstration of power off the Norwegian coast, and to crush any convoys in the area. His movements were reported to the Admiralty by the Intelligence Department, and the Grand Fleet left Scapa Flow, the great naval base in the Orkney Islands, to make contact. This was first done by light cruisers, and Admiral Beatty with the battle cruisers engaged those of the Imperial Fleet, under Admiral Hipper, at about four in the afternoon of May 31.

Those great warships, armed like battleships. but with higher speed (up to 30 knots as against 21 knots), were networks of mechanized operation. Telephones, electrical devices, mechanical gun training, and calculation for ranges, provided the greatest accumulation of technical apparatus to that date. Where the old *Monitor* of 1862 had to retire from action while the turret was rotated to align with the magazine trunk, the gun turret of 1916 had a feed trunk revolving with the turret. As the shell and charge came in turn up the lift, a great hydraulic ram uncoiled itself to push them into the breech. On discharge, the huge 100-ton gun slid smoothly back and out again, the stupendous recoil absorbed by the hydraulic system. No longer did unbearable noise blast back into the turret, for white canvas covers (*breeches* or *blast rags*) were around the barrels to cover the embrasures. However, the concussion was still terrific, even though the guns were fired only in salvoes (one at a time from each turret). Seamen in the control tops and upper-deck positions were often thrown about in their cramped quarters, with some bruising.

There was much variation in the main armament of the Royal Navy's biggest ships in the 1914 war. Most of the older vessels, going back to the *Majestic* class of 1895, had 12-inch guns. *Swiftsure*, of 1902, had 10-inch, the *Iron Duke* class of 1914 had 13.5-inch, and the 1913—15 classes like *Queen Elizabeth* and *Renown* had 15-inch guns. All these weapons were 45 to 50 calibers long, e.g., the 12-inch 45-caliber type was 45 feet long. Only the seamen serving the heaviest guns were protected by stout armor; the secondary armament had relatively little shielding.

Admiral Beatty's battle cruisers sustained much damage shortly after fire was opened. As the youngest navy, German seamen had concentrated their utmost efforts on gunnery, with dire effect at Jutland. Within a few minutes, *Lion*, *Princess Royal*, and *Tiger* were hit, then *Indefatigable* engaged *Von der Tann*. A salvo of three 11-inch shells dropped squarely on the British vessel, by the forward turret. As she began to go down, a further salvo created a frightful internal explosion, and a few moments later *Indefatigable* rolled and sank. Twenty minutes after that catastrophe, *Queen Mary* opposed *Seydlitz* and *Derfflinger*. Twelve-inch shells from the latter straddled the Royal Navy ship, then *Derfflinger* hit with a salvo forward. Even in daylight the scarlet flame blazed up vividly, and she was torn by a terrific explosion below decks. Funnels and masts vanished, an

161

enormous hole gaped on the starboard side, and at once *Queen Mary* turned right over. Everything happened so quickly that *Tiger*, following astern, plunged through the cloud of smoke, and debris from *Queen Mary* fell upon *Tiger*'s deck.

Little more than an hour later, the British battleships were

BATTLE CRUISER 'DERFFLINGER'

SURRENDER OF GERMAN FLEET, NOVEMBER 1918.

on the scene, firing as they came. Under the rain of 15-inch shells, the German battle cruisers suffered heavily. Hipper tried to escape around the end of the British line, but he found himself heading for the center, with the horizon on either side a flashing arc of gunfire. With a strange mental reaction, he signalled: "Charge the enemy. Ram. Attack without regard to consequences." This was suicidal before

162

the might of the battleships' guns; the German vessels could not get nearer than 9,000 yards, at terrific cost. Scheer finally countermanded Hipper's order, and recalled him to the main battle line in retreat.

Admiral Jellicoe's fleet movements placed his force between Scheer and home, but during the night the latter made a daring thrust through his enemy's destroyer screen and reached port. In the matter of numbers, the Germans could claim supremacy, for they had destroyed 14 British ships against a loss of 11. Nevertheless, Admiral Jellicoe was cruising unchallenged on the German coast. In fact, the Imperial Fleet was never again in action.

When the war was drawing to a close, with defeat staring the Germans in the face, naval preparations were made for a desperate "death or glory" attack upon the British fleet, at the end of October, 1918. Morale was low; there was still the cleavage between officers and seamen, in the old Prussian tradition. This prevented any rallying or inspiring of the navy, such as would probably have taken place where there was *rapport* between the rank levels. Poor food had sapped the seamen's energies, and fostered extreme discontent. On October 29, a rumbling of mutiny burst into explosion, when the stokers of two battleships drew fires and refused duty. A Red Flag was flying from every warship by November 7, while Kiel and Wilhelmshaven were controlled by the Soviet of Workers, Soldiers, and Sailors. On shore, the *Internationale* resounded in the street, and naval stores were openly looted.

At the Armistice meeting, on November 11, 1918, the Allied Premiers agreed that all the 160 German submarines should be surrendered, and that the High Seas Fleet, with all naval forces, should be interned. Accordingly, on November 21, the most remarkable naval spectacle ever seen was staged on the North Sea. Allied warships were drawn up in a double line, and down the lane thus formed came majestically the

163

naval forces of Imperial Germany, sailing to internment in
Scapa Flow. Their standards were flown until sunset of that
fatal day, and then struck for ever.

During the long peace negotiations of 1919, Admiral von
Reuter was in charge of the fleet, wherein a number of
seamen had become Bolsheviks. He concluded that, if no
agreement was reached, it was his duty to prevent the ships

EARLY R.N.
AIRCRAFT
CARRIERS

'FURIOUS'
CONVERTED 1917.

'EAGLE', COMPLETED 1923.

from being taken over by the Allies. Von Reuter gained that
impression on June 21, so he hoisted a secret signal, and
aboard every ship the seacocks were opened. Despite frantic
British efforts to counter the move, 50 of the 72 warships
went to the bottom, the remainder being beached.

Scapa Flow is a lonely place now. Its wide stretch of water
is almost entirely devoid of shipping, but some memorials to

that gallant gesture still lie rusting on the seabed. Many of the ships were salvaged between 1924 and 1932.

Among the new features developed around the British seaman during the war was the naval aircraft. In 1912 the Royal Naval Air Service had been established, and the Navy Estimates of February, 1914 included the sum of £81,000, to provide a ship "for carrying aeroplanes." A merchantman was bought and converted as *Ark Royal* (later *Pegasus*), with a 103-foot flight deck and stowage for ten seaplanes. Cranes were fitted for hoisting the aircraft inboard. When war broke out, an old cruiser, *Hermes*, and six cross-Channel steamers were set up with flight decks, stowage and cranes. From one of the steamers, *Engadine*, a seaplane took off to reconnoiter for the battle cruisers at Jutland.

When the role of the flying seaman was established, the Cunard liner *Campania* was rebuilt with a 230-foot flight deck, along which the seaplane taxied with trucks under the floats. At first the pilot himself detached the trucks when airborne, but an automatic release was devised with deckgear. Land aircraft were obviously best in service, but the difficult problem of landing on the carrier was an obstacle. For this reason, in November 1917, the 18-inch gun cruiser *Furious* was rebuilt as the first true aircraft carrier.

Naturally the technique of landing on a deck was a special skill to be developed, and there were disasters at first. Tranverse wires on the deck engaged hooks on the undercarriage, but the degree of tension was difficult to gauge. At one time arrester gear was abandoned altogether, and the aircraft were checked by seamen and Royal Flying Corps personnel, who dragged on the wing tips. After the war, it was decided that the Air Ministry could not cope with the special requirements of the seamen's air fleet, so the Fleet Air Arm was created (1924–25). It was jointly administered by the Admiralty and the Royal Air Force.

Though the United States Navy took no major part in

naval action during the war, it supplied a number of much-needed destroyers for convoy work. From the shipping industry came a stream of mass-produced cargo ships and destroyers to neutralize U-boat sinkings. Loring Swasey of Boston redesigned the coastal motor torpedo boats used by the Allies, and nearly 450 of these were in action against

SEAMAN, RUSSIAN BLACK SEA FLEET, 1917.

submarines. They were fitted with the improved hydrophone developed by Captain Leigh, U.S. Submarine Headquarters. Extensive minelaying was done by Americans in northern waters, between Norway and Scotland, and it was considered that by October 1918 one U-boat in five struck a mine.

Throughout the period of hostilities, the Russian fleet was largely ineffectual. Though six new battleships were launched in 1914, the seamen had not recovered from the effects of the 1905 disasters. There were no up-to-date submarines, and few destroyers. No ship could carry more than four days' coal, and winter coaling at sea was impossible. Some uplift was given by an alliance with Japan in 1916, when the Japs returned three warships taken as prizes in 1905. Russian troops were actually conveyed to the Western Front in Japanese ships. It is significant that seamen were to the forefront in the street fighting of the Revolution. They had suffered far more than the workers or the soldiers, in being confined aboard under lofty and tyrannical officers, and subjected to the most appalling conditions. In October, 1917, the cruiser *Aurora*, from Kronstadt, shelled the Winter Palace and the Admiralty—the seaman striking at the regime that had oppressed him.

12

Seafaring Life and Lifesaving

When the world emerged from the black pit of the war, it was
to find that "the old order changeth." Though seamanship
was the means of directing and looking after a ship, those
who did this were far in the minority aboard. This was
particularly so in the age of the great passenger liners, in
which the crew included a number of purely domestic
workers with no knowledge at all in the craft of the sea. In
the same way, the technicians, such as engineers, electricians
and radio operators, did not need to be seamen. Even those
crew members with deck duties, who maintained the
lifeboats and operated the davits, had no occasion for
seamanship.

A scientific age had brought to the sea a most valuable
shipping aid in the radio installation, which had been
developed for commercial vessels since its use aboard
warships in 1900. In January 1909, the American liner
Republic collided with the Italian *Florida*, some miles south
of the Nantucket Light, in the north Atlantic. As *Republic*
had a radio set she was able to call for help, bringing to her
three other radio-fitted ships in the area. Such a telling
example caused a number of shipping companies to fit up
their vessels as a safety measure.

By the middle 1930s, international law had made wireless
fitments compulsory for passenger vessels, at least. Safety
was the main object, both as regards personnel and ship.
Apart from help calls, the ship could send and receive

weather reports, and could check her chronometer. A radio direction finder provided guidance in fog, as well as giving a *fix* for position. For these reasons the radio gear was permanently manned on watch, to be ready for incoming signals. Further application of electrical sound was made in the depth-finding gear, where a series of waves were reflected

STOKEHOLD OF COAL-FIRED SHIP   Above: In oil-fired ship.

back from the seabed and amplified to check the time lag. Amplifiers were used, too, in communication thoughout the ship, to address crew or passengers.

Another increasing change on shipboard was in the stokehold, the place of the "black gang." Soon after the war, oil firing began to take the place of coal, with all its attendant filth and heat wastage. On oil-burning ships, a

169

F*

spray of heavy oil was consumed in burners to heat the boilers, so that the men responsible for the operation had but to work a lever. In this way the first of the mechanized processes was reorganized, and by 1930 a further step had been made in developing large-scale electric propulsion. This was seen to advantage in the great French liner *Normandie*, 80,000 tons, which was launched in 1932.

If a seaman of a hundred years before could have stepped into the crew's quarters on a luxury liner, they would seem like a palace compared to his own damp and smelly forecastle berth. Perhaps a thousand crew members were accommodated, all decently provided for, with comfortable bunks, recreation areas, good food and entertainment. That great French ship, like a floating city with her 1,000-foot hull, dwarfed anything that the seaman of 1832 could have seen.

Normandie was rivalled and finally beaten in the contest for the fastest Atlantic crossing by the Cunard Line *Queen Mary* of 1936 (81,237 tons). A sister ship, *Queen Elizabeth* (82,997 tons), was launched in 1938, and both luxury liners served as troopships in the 1940s. Cunard's immense steamship empire was badly hit by a merchant seamen's strike in 1966. It lasted from mid-May to early July, over a question of pay and hours. At that time, the seaman averaged £20 a week (56 hours). Nothing was gained by the strike, though it led to congestion and double banking of moored ships in the great ports.

In general, the public felt little effect, as there were plentiful supplies in the country—including a year's supply of fuel. Hundreds of thousands of pounds in wages were lost by the seamen during the strike period, and this lost pay could never be recouped. They did gain a reduction to a 48-hour week, with 6s. an hour for overtime, but it was definitely not a victory. More serious still were the effects on the Cunard Line, which lost millions.

This led to the sale of the great Queen liners to American

buyers as show vessels and floating hotels. The *Queen Mary* was sold for £1,230,000 (about $3,444,000.00) and she left England for ever on October 31, 1967. By April, 1968 the *Queen Elizabeth* had been sold for £3,500,000 (about $8,400,000.00) and was ready to follow. Four other liners were sold by Cunard at the same time, but in September, 1968 they launched *Queen Elizabeth II.* This was a smaller vessel than either of the first Queens; she was rated at 65,000 tons, and the cost—£29,500,000 (about $70,800,000.00)—was partly provided by the British Government.

Ship rating in the twentieth century is defined in clear divisions. *Gross tonnage* is the most commonly-used figure for passenger and cargo vessels. This shows the enclosed volume of the ship at 100 cubic feet to the ton, less a few unconsidered spaces. In connection with this rating, *net tonnage* represents the volume of actual passenger and cargo space. Oil tankers and ore-carrying ships are measured by their cargo capacity in *tons deadweight.* In that case the weight of the ship with all fittings is deducted from the weight of water displaced by the loaded ship, when the water level is at the Summer Load Line draft indicator on the hull. *Tons displacement* is employed when gauging warships, being the amount of water displaced when the vessel is equipped and manned, having aboard all stores but fuel oil.

Though the 1930s saw the great development of powered ships, there were a number of interesting survivals, where true seamanship of the old type was required. These were largely coasters, small fore-and-aft vessels such as the ketch and the topsail schooner, many hailing from Portmadoc, in Carnarvonshire, North Wales. This little port lived by its coasters, though a number belied the name by trading at a distance. A well-known round voyage was the Baltic run with a cargo of slate, bringing back bottles in return.

Crew quarters on the Welsh coasters were of the old type,

where the seamen slept in berths with sliding shutters to save them from falling out, if the ship were lively. Other coasters provided iron-framed bunks hinged to the side, but defective caulking often resulted in leaky decks and discomfort below. On most of these little ships the pumps were overworked, as the heavy cargoes they carried through wild water tended to strain their timbers. Some masters employed the "Blackwall caulk," letting the loaded ship take a muddy berth, so that mud was forced between her planks to back up the pitch-and-oakum caulking. (Oakum was loose fiber from old pieces of rope, a time-honored caulking material. Picking oakum was once an occupation for convicts.)

Sailing coasters, usually ketches with auxiliary engines, were once a common sight in the Bristol Channel, plying between north Devon and Cornwall ports and South Wales. Not many such vessels survived the 1930 decade, and the same can be said of the great full-rigged ships. One of the most famous of the sailing survivals was the *Hertzogin Cecilie*, with a gross tonnage of 3,111 tons. She was a German-built steel craft, launched in 1902, and she rated as a four-masted bark, through having a fore-and-aft topsail on the *jigger* (aftermost mast).

Originally this fine vessel was a cadet trainer, so there were no reef points on her sails, nor any laborsaving gear such as brace and halyard winches. Her crew of 60 cadets could make light of the work. When she became a cargo carrier, in the Finnish fleet of Gustav Erikson, she had only 25 crew at the most. This gained for her the name of "a proper workhouse." *Hertzogin Cecilie* served her owner well, but her useful career was cut short in 1936, when she ran on the rocks of the south Devon coast, at Salcombe.

Some "tall ships" were still extant in the late 1960s, in use as trainers; the British-built *Sir Winston Churchill*, and *Malcolm Miller* were launched by the Sail Training Association during that period. Another kind of sail survival

172

was shown in commemorative replicas built and sailed across the Atlantic. *Santa Maria* was the first of these, in 1892, while at least two Viking longships have been built and taken

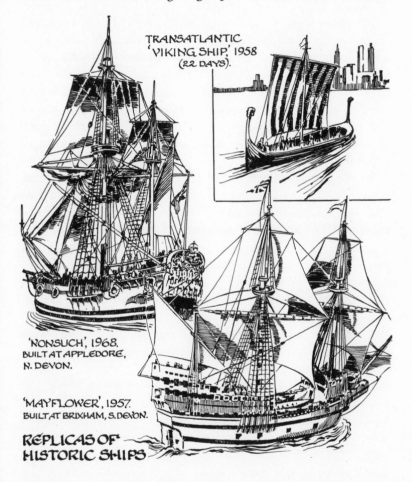

TRANSATLANTIC
'VIKING SHIP', 1958
(22 DAYS).

'NONSUCH', 1968.
BUILT AT APPLEDORE,
N. DEVON.

'MAYFLOWER', 1957.
BUILT AT BRIXHAM, S. DEVON.

REPLICAS OF
HISTORIC SHIPS

across—one in the early 1930s and another in 1958. *Mayflower* was built at Brixham in Devon, to make the voyage in 1963, and in 1968 a further Devonshire contribution was a replica of the ketch *Nonsuch*, launched at the Appledore shipyard in North Devon. She represented the first ship sent out by the merchants who had founded the Hudson's Bay Company under the patronage of Prince Rupert in 1670.

All these replicas were constructed with the most careful attention to detail, and ancient techniques such as adzwork were employed. It is true that the 1963 *Mayflower* had a wheel instead of a whipstaff. On inquiring about this, the author was advised by a London newspaper that the wheel had been requested, to make the voyage easier.

These undertakings served to keep alive the ancient spirit of seamanship, overlaid as it was by mechanical devices in all other respects.

In the remarkable story of men at sea, there is one great service that is nobler than all others rendered by the crew of the lifeboat when the sea threatens death. Apparently a coachbuilder named Lionel Lukin, of Long Acre, in London, constructed the first known lifeboat in 1784. He bought a Norwegian yawl (a two-masted, fore-and-aft coaster type) which he fitted with a cork belt tapering from nine inches thickness amidships. A number of watertight compartments were arranged, and Lukin added a stability keel of iron. Several successful lifeboats were fitted up in this way, but despite the lives they saved, no general move was made to establish coastal rescue units.

At last, in March, 1789, the townsmen of South Shields, in Durham, were shocked into activity by the wreck of the Newcastle tradeship *Adventure* on a dangerous sandbank in Tyne mouth. *Adventure*'s hapless crew dropped from the rigging one by one, into the huge breakers, before the horrified eyes of a great crowd. A gentleman's club in the vicinity offered a two-guinea award for ideas on a lifeboat. William Wouldhave, a house painter and singing master, submitted a model which became the basis of another by two club members, Fairles and Rockwood. A boatbuilder

Henry Greathead, was employed to produce the 30-foot *Original*. It was double-ended, like a whaler, and as it was steered by an oar over the stern, it could be rowed either way. A feature of the design was a curved keel, and buoyancy was maintained by a cork lining a foot thick. On each gunwale was a 21-foot cork fender secured by copper bands. There were seven hundredweights of cork in all, but no airtight boxes, and she could only be cleared of water by baling.

THE COXSWAIN

PULLING LIFEBOAT RESCUE:
Rocket line aboard.

Hundreds of lives were saved by *Original*, which continued in service until 1830, when she broke in two on a rocky ridge. By 1803 Greathead had built 31 boats, eight being for export, but there was no organized administration of the service.

Every phase of the early lifeboat's story was introduced by disaster. It was the sight of appalling wrecks and drowning seamen off the Isle of Man that impelled Sir William Hillary to found the Royal National Lifeboat Institution, in 1824.

175

Hillary gave active help to save over 300 lives in Douglas Bay, and three times he gained the Institution's gold medal for gallantry. In one case, where the new lifeboat was not quite ready for use, Hillary went out to the wreck of the Royal Mail *St. George* in a conventional boat, with two friends and a crew of 14. He was one of four who were washed overboard

SIR WILLIAM HILLARY.

and had to be rescued, Hillary with his chest crushed and six broken ribs. However, the gallant venture saved every life on *St. George*.

In most cases, lifeboat crews were composed of coastal seamen and fishermen. A pulling boat presented the bitterest strain on muscles and stamina, in that it was launched into breakers, the most difficult rowing situation. Only sheer devotion to the task of rescue could bring men into the service, so it meant that they were the cream of the seafaring community.

During the middle nineteenth century, a type of pulling boat was developed to remain the standard for many years. It was self-righting, by virtue of large flotation boxes with turtle backs, at bow and stern, a watertight deck raised well above the keel, and inboard air-cases. In a 33-foot, ten-oared boat, the buoyancy equalled 11½ tons, and if the boat capsized, eight hundredweights of ballast and a nine-ton iron keel rolled it back to upright. When the boat filled, six discharge tubes with one-way valves cleared the water in about half a minute. Boats of this size could take 30 people in addition to the crew.

Excellent support in rescue operations was given by shore apparatus, such as mortar and rocket lines fired to the wreck. Captain G.W. Manby, of the Royal Navy, produced the original form of rocket line in 1807, and John Dennett, of Newport, Isle of Wight, contributed work which resulted in the *breeches buoy*, about 1830. This comprised a heavy line hauled across after the light rocket line, and rove through tackle on a mast. With a similar device at the shore end, an endless cable was provided. On that a traveller block was slung, having below it a lifebelt forming the top of a large pair of canvas breeches. Each person got into the breeches and was drawn ashore by a line attached to the movable gear.

An American life-saving service was first established by the Humane Society of Massachusetts about 1798, when shelter huts and rescue boats were disposed along the coast. By 1848 the U.S. Government was persuaded to take action, through the work of Congressman W.A. Newell of New Jersey, in the House of Representatives. Before long, Captain Douglass Ottinger, in command of the United States Life-Saving Service, introduced his *life car*, an enclosed amphibious vessel with an entry manhole. This protected rescued people while they were being drawn ashore through surf. It was especially useful for invalids and children.

English-type lifeboats were too heavy for the flat beaches

177

around the coast, so surfboats were used. Though these were not self-righting or self-clearing, the crews were so expert in handling them that the boats served well. Under provisions of 1871, a chain of stations was set up, with patrols between them, and amenities such as libraries were arranged for the seamen on duty.

Next in line with life-saving associations were France and Germany. These were set up by both countries in 1865, the French service using English-type apparatus and methods. In

STEAM & MOTOR LIFEBOAT TYPES

the French mercantile marine, one of the qualifications for a captain's command was efficiency in the management of life-saving gear. Every ship in the French navy was equipped with a line-throwing mortar—this was preferred to the rocket. German life squads based their system on the American-style light craft, as their coastal regions were flat and sandy. Their boats were reinforced with iron plating, and were almost impossible to capsize.

Until 1890, all British lifeboats were propelled by strong arms and heartbreaking toil, but in that year the first powered lifeboat came into service—the *Duke of Northumberland*, stationed at Harwich. At first, much in the minority, these steam lifeboats and the motorized types that followed (1903) increased in numbers, to displace by degrees the old pulling and sailing craft. In 1936, the relative numbers were 128 powered boats to 41 pulling, and by 1948 only two pulling boats were left.

Motorized lifeboats of the middle 1930s were well equipped, with tracer line-throwing guns, radiotelephones, searchlights, Morse lamps, and sprayers to spread oil over rough water. Other gear might include fire-extinguishing appliances, rescue haul ropes, and a *drogue* or sea anchor to keep the boat from *broaching-to*—coming broadside on to the seas in heavy surf. Most up-to-date vessels are not self-righting, as such designs are more difficult to handle. Nonrighters are built so broad in the beam that capsizing is most unlikely. When they ship water, they are cleared by a system of scuppers. In a roll, the downside scuppers open and the upper sides close, while all scuppers are open when the boat is on an even keel.

A new type of self-righter was tried at Littlehampton, Sussex, in 1958. Shifting water ballast passed through a pair of pipes between ballast tanks, bringing a capsized boat upright in six seconds. The success at Littlehampton was followed by another innovation—an inshore inflatable minilifeboat of Neoprene nylon, with a crew of two and space for eight other people. It was powered by a 44 h.p. outboard motor, which gave 20 knots. Such a craft proved invaluable for coastal rescue work when it began service in the summer of 1963. On 20-foot waves it could go over to 90°, for its side buoyancy tubes returned it to level. By 1968 there were nearly 150 of these high-speed rescue boats around the seaside resorts of Britain. They were manned by amateur seamen of all kinds—policemen, factory workers, photographers and bank clerks.

Fishermen formed the backbone of the lifeboat service from its beginnings, and many of these expert seamen were prominent in another form of lifesaving during the Great War of 1914. Great numbers of fishermen were in the Royal Naval Reserve, which was recruited entirely from the Merchant Navy and coastal seamen. In the Reserve, a special

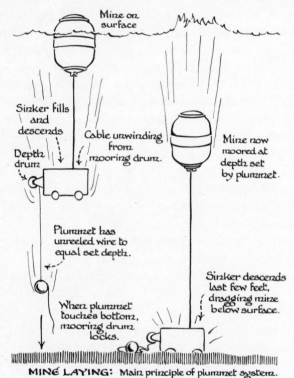

MINE LAYING: Main principle of plummet system.

Trawler Section was formed in 1912. This detachment became responsible for minesweeping, the hazardous task that kept open vital shipping lanes.

Sea mines were sown to stay beneath the surface, by means of depth-setting gear. One type was thrown overside on a little truck, which sank and unwound from a drum the
180

mooring line attached to the mine. Below the truck hung a heavy ball on a line of set length, and this ball touched the seabed first. When that happened, the mooring drum stopped turning, and locked the line. Though the truck continued to sink, no more line was unwound, so the floating mine was pulled below the surface until it was held at the set depth, when the truck landed on the seabed. In the mine itself, a series of horn detonators set off the main charge on contact.

A minesweeper's function was to bring mines to the surface, where they could be exploded, usually by rifle fire striking the horns. At first, in 1914, pairs of ships towed between them cutter-bearing lines that severed the mooring cables of the mines. In 1915 the *paravane* was first devised, a towing device shaped like an aircraft. One was towed on each side of the sweeper, so that the cutter bracket and serrated blade on the paravane's nose engaged and cut the mooring cables.

13

Again the Struggle

When the effects of the 1914 war had passed, the seaman of the Royal Navy in the middle 1930s enjoyed conditions aboard that made the old-time Navy look like penal servitude. Especially noticeable was the excellence of the victualling service. Instead of the cramped, insanitary galley, ruled by a hit-or-miss ship's cook, the largest ships had roomy kitchens and bakeries. Even a destroyer's kitchen equalled that of the smaller restaurant ashore, with refrigerator storage.

Food preparation was done by skilled seamen trained in the Royal Naval School of Cookery, and one might well compare the palatable meals with the old burgoo, biscuit (with weevils) and salt junk. A typical day's food was a bacon-and-egg breakfast: veal and ham pie, with vegetables, and a fruit dessert, at midday: butter and jam for tea, and a supper of corned beef, with coffee. While in port, bread was bought ashore, but at sea it was baked on board. There was an unforgettable appetizing smell from the scores of new loaves in the bakery.

Hammocks were still slung in the 'tweendecks, but no stuffy, dank quarters were to be seen—ample ventilation and lighting, with well-equipped recreation areas. Each man had as a basic issue his locker, his *ditty box* for small personal items, and his hammock with the bedroll. Messing was organized by grouping men with the same duties—stokers and seamen in their separate messes, and Royal Marines in their "barracks" at the after end of the mess-decks.

Even at the time of Jutland provisions for medical treatment and surgery on board left much to be desired. A surviving description tells of the casualty theater in a light cruiser engaged in the battle:

"The operating room was the stokers' bathroom . . . a small room that the shoregoer would hesitate to use as a darkroom to his house, it might get so stuffy. The size of this room was about eight feet high, twelve feet broad, and twelve feet long. The center of the room was occupied by a light portable operating table."

In that little place the two ship's doctors dealt with 50 seriously wounded after a few minutes engagement in the battle. Naval doctors, as noncombatants, were exposed to the same perils as the crew, for there could be no Red Cross protection for them while in action. This could not be altered, but 20 years made a great difference to the layout and facilities of the ship's sick bay and operating theater.

Daily routine on board was in keeping with the traditions of the Navy—cocoa at 5.30 a.m. for the watch on deck, from six to seven deck scrubbing, with breakfast at seven. At eight o'clock (nine in winter) the colors were hoisted with impressive ceremony, an ages-old naval rite. Eight bells were struck for the end of the watch, the Royal Marines buglers sounded "Attention," and the watch faced aft while the officers stood at the salute. As the colors moved up to break out on the staff, the Marines band played the National Anthem.

Inspection took place at 9 a.m., with the watch mustered in divisions, and a brief assembly was held. For the rest of the forenoon, maintenance and routine ship-cleaning went on, with the boys and young seamen in the schoolroom. At noon came the ancient ceremony of the grog issue, though by the middle 1930s many seamen accepted pay (3d. a day) instead. This was followed by the midday meal, and work recommenced at 1.15 p.m.—bright work, gun cleaning, the scores of tasks that kept the ship trim and in good order.

On Saturdays and Sundays routine work was reduced to a minimum, with traditional "make and mend" periods. These were originally granted for seamen to do actual tailoring or repairs, but for the twentieth century seaman they were off-duty spells for recreation.

There had been some changes in the nature of the uniform since the early years of the century. Until 1906, the 1891 dress had been worn—No. 1 being a blue serge frock, with gold badges, worn with the square collar and cloth trousers. Except for red badges, No. 2 was the same dress, while No. 3 had serge trousers instead of cloth. Also on issue were the white work jumper, duck trousers, check shirt and white drill frock, worn in various combinations according to the number of the dress. Under the 1906 order, No. 2 with blue serge jumper took the place of the old-type frock as No. 1, except in the Royal yacht crew's rig. With the new No. 1 dress, still called a frock by the seamen despite the order, there were cuffs with two buttons, and an inside pocket on the left. When No. 1 became shabby, the cuffs and red badges were taken off, and it became a "Stepney," No. 2; only then did the men call it a jumper. For dirty work, boiler suits of the blue jean or canvas were issued, but the 1891 "monkey jacket" as outer wear was discontinued.

An order of 1934 abolished the seaman's old-type square neck handkerchief of black which had to be carefully folded and tied in regulation style. In its place was issued a scarf form, with sewn loop ends to be caught by tapes passed through the jumper.

During the War, in 1917, the Women's Royal Naval Service (Wrens) was founded. In this unit, the rating was extinguished in a voluminous, shapeless serge frock, buttoned high. This was modified by the ratings themselves, who cut the neck lower, and filled it in with a white flannel front. A

184

seaman's collar of small size was part of the dress, though
many ratings preferred the regulation collar. Their hats were
of gabardine, pleated on the crown, with stitching in the brim
to stiffen it. In summer a white hat cover was issued, but no
other change was made—black shoes and stockings were

1917   1942

W. R. N. S. RATINGS

retained for summer. In 1919 the Wrens were disbanded, to
be reformed twenty years later.

Since the mechanization of the Navy began, the rise of the
technician had become progressively more noticeable. In the
1930 decade, it was most marked; a two-stream entry into
the Royal Navy was fully established. Under this scheme a
boy could enter as a seaman boy or an engine-room
apprentice. Shipbuilding apprentices who had served their

185

time could go straight into the Navy as volunteer engine-room artificers. They were ranked as petty officers, with 9s. a day.

At that time, the basic pay of an able seaman was 4s. 6d. a day, while ordinary seamen received 2s. 9d. Allowances were given for various specialities such as gunnery or signalling, and each good conduct badge gained 3d. a day. For the seaman, the normal road of promotion was from petty officer to chief p.o. at 10s. a day, and thence to warrant officer beginning at 12s. 6d. From 1912, it had been possible to reach commissioned rank by passing through grades of "mate." Between 1913 and 1930 over 450 "lowerdeck" commissions were granted, and under a revised scheme the engine-room personnel were brought in. An old-time seaman would describe this progress as "aft through the hawsehole."

During several days in mid-September, 1931, some disturbing incidents occurred, which have been styled "the Invergordon mutiny." It was brought about by the Government's economy measures in the financial crisis of that period. Cuts were made in the lower deck pay, between 10 per cent and 13 per cent overall, which aroused great resentment. A large crowd of ratings, chiefly from H.M.S. *Rodney*, held meetings ashore in Invergordon on three occasions, and some damage was done. Canteen furniture and windows were smashed, though there was no ugly incident. In fact, after one meeting, the seamen retired singing "The more we are together," a popular song known as "The Frothblowers' Anthem." All shore leave was stopped, the various units of the Fleet were dispersed to their home ports, and Fleet exercises were abandoned until feelings simmered down.

This was a period of most serious discussion between the great powers of the interwar years, regarding the future of the battleship. Long before, Admiral Sir Percy Scott had shaken the Service world by declaring against the capital ship in view of the undersea menace. A further threat to the great ship was the warplane. Naval power above and under the sea appeared likely to counter power on the sea.

In America, during the Presidency of Warren Harding (1921–23), disarmament had been discussed, and the Secretary of State, Charles E. Hughes, was in favor of confining warships to 10,000 tons, with 8-inch guns. A strong body of opinion in Congress decried all peacetime naval

RATING PILOTS, c.1936.

forces, on the grounds of American tradition, but the lesson of the 1914–18 war was too recent to be ignored.

In order to keep abreast of developments, the naval air base at Pensacola, Florida, was expanded to become the principal station. An increase of 5 per cent in pay attracted young men to the base, and it is claimed that dive-bombing originated there, in support of Marines landing exercises. A tragic aspect of Naval air training was the post-1918 work with dirigibles (airships). Several were built in America and Germany for the U.S. Navy but all seem to have been lost.

187

Shenandoah of 1923 split apart in a flight over Ohio two years later, and shortly after that *Akron* plunged into the sea. She took down with her Rear-Admiral W.A. Moffet, one of the great founders of naval aviation. *Macon* was wrecked through structural failure in 1935, which finally placed a check on airship building.

Nevertheless, in the interwar period, the U.S. Navy underwent a considerable build-up, with attention to aircraft carriers as a major item. At that stage the force ran neck-and-neck with the Royal Navy as to strength, though there was an American lead in carriers. While the development was going on, Adolf Hitler's influence in Germany brought a revival of militarism that pervaded the whole nation. Under the Versailles Pact of 1919, Germany was forbidden to build submarines, or to have any warship over 10,000 tons. Pact restrictions were being openly broken or sidestepped by 1930. U-boats were being built, and under Hitler (1934) Germany acquired warships within the tonnage limit, but carrying 11-inch guns. Normally a ship of 10,000 tons mounted six-inch or eight-inch guns. Those units of the new German navy were called "pocket battleships." By an agreement of 1935, Germany was permitted naval strength equal to 35 per cent of the Royal Navy.

When Britain declared war on Germany on Sunday, September 3,1939, she did so in support of a defense pact with Poland. Britain's chief power was on the sea, yet Poland had no seaboard whatever—simply the concession port of Danzig, in Prussian territory. A defense pact under those conditions seemed most unwise.

As matters then stood, British seamen saw the clock put back 25 years. Merchant fleets were again in peril, and Britain's survival depended on keeping open the sea lanes. Only a few hours after the declaration of war, a U-boat, evidently stationed off the Irish coast to await the outbreak, torpedoed the Donaldson Atlantic liner *Athenia*, with over

1,400 people aboard. No warning was given, and two witnessess, the captain and a deck storehand, testified that the attacker fired at least one shell at the stricken ship. Nearly 400 lives were lost.

When conducting the new U-boat war, the raiders usually moved in packs, with a special technique. They lay in line a mile or two apart, on either side of a slow convoy's course, and at night the inner units fired torpedoes into the thick of the merchantmen. Those U-boats on the wings moved ahead to take the inner station on the next night's attack, while their fellows came after them to lie on the outside. During daylight the submarines travelled on the surface, at twice the speed of the convoy, and out of sight. This method only permitted U-boat coverage of certain areas, but the German authorities thought it more effective than scattering the attackers singly at wider range.

A remarkable killer campaign against U-boats was conducted by Captain F.J. Walker, in his sloop *Starling*, launched in 1942. She became famous as the ace killer, for Captain Walker had an original approach when leading his Second Escort Group. He called it the "creeping depth charge," a trail of charges sent down by a line of ships covering the suspected area at five knots, in relative silence. Captain Walker died after 18 months on this service, owing to the intolerable strain of his efforts.

During the desperate struggle at sea, U-boat designers concentrated on the problem of restricted air supplies when submerged. This had a bad effect when the vessel was forced to hover, or travel submerged for a long period of time while being hunted. Her crew began to sag and pant for air; their endurance below at full speed was only two hours, though a low speed extended this period considerably. Shortage of oxygen gave the seamen severe headaches, besides making them sick and listless. Occasionally, submarines on both sides carried cylinders of oxygen for emergency use, but pure

189

oxygen is really unsuitable for the purpose. In British submarines trays of soda lime were laid out throughout the vessel, to absorb carbon dioxide, but to be fully effective it needed a circulation of air through the absorbent.

For many U-boats those conditions were relieved by the invention of the *schnorkel*, a telescopic air intake and exhaust combined, which permitted the diesels to be run below. It was first made known to the public in November, 1944, and a record was achieved by U977 when escaping to South America in 1945. She was submerged for 66 days.

Germany's surface war could not be very effective when her forces were opposed to the giant naval strength of Britain, so her warships carried on the ignoble work of commerce raiding. In December 1940, the pocket battleship *Graf Spee* was cornered in the South Atlantic by a cruiser squadron under Commodore Harwood, in *Exeter*, with H.M.S. *Ajax* and H.M.N.Z.S. *Achilles*. *Exeter* led the attack, running the gauntlet of *Graf Spee*'s 11-inch guns to get her own eight-inch within range. Her consorts, with their six-inch guns, backed her up nobly. Though the German raider inflicted considerable damage on *Exeter*, she herself was forced to withdraw into Montevideo for repairs. Reinforcements were drawn up in the estuary of the River Plate, making escape impossible, so *Graf Spee* was fired and scuttled by Hitler's direct order.

At this point the Royal Navy had reached the peak of organization and training. A warship on active service presented a highly complex pattern of co-operative effort, whose climax was the delivery of offensive fire. In the Director Control Tower, the Gunnery Lieutenant presided over a vital team. On each side sat observers, the Spotting Officer on his left to check the fall of shells, on his right a petty officer noting the rate at which the range altered. Before "Guns" sat the chief petty officer who actually fired the guns with a push-button.

With the C.P.O. were a group of ratings, each with an important task calling for reliability of the highest order. Three range takers viewed the objective as a double image on their range finders, to be brought into one by adjusting turnscrews. This caused indicators to point to a figure, in yards, on the range scale. It was read off aloud, e.g. "Range five-eight-oh." Other ratings operated sensitive instruments which adjusted the angle and direction of the guns as required, while the telephone rating dealt with incoming calls.

All signals passed through the Transmitting Station deep down in the ship's hull, where the Royal Marines bandsmen had the duty of looking after the delicate instruments there. For instance, the findings of the three range takers were averaged and employed with greater speed than a human brain could achieve. Estimates from the other observers in Director Control were received and applied to the task of lining up a moving target from a moving platform. There were instruments that allowed for wind force, variations in air conditions, and the heating up of the guns.

In turrets with guns up to six-inch caliber, the shells were manhandled from the carrier hoists. These passed through a series of flash-tight doorways on the way from the magazine, to avoid transmitting fire if the turret were hit. For each shot a primer tube was inserted, to be fired by electrical contact from the Director Tower. When the breech was re-opened, a fierce gust of compressed air swept the bore, like the old water clearance. A six-inch gun could be served at one shot in ten seconds, with a 100-pound shell, while a 16-inch fired a one-ton shell once in 25 seconds. Fire control was exercised by a three-button signal, "over," "short," or "hit." It was vital that each turret commander observed the fall of his own shells correctly, in view of continual adjustment by Control. When a hit was registered, it showed in a brief yellow flash.

Oil-burning ships had the advantage of producing smoke

191

screens at will. This was most valuable in protecting a convoy from surface attack, for no enemy ship would steer blindly into the screen. Smoke was made by cutting down the burners in the furnaces, so that they did not properly consume the spray of oil fuel. It was possible for the defensive units to emerge from cover, deliver torpedoes or a burst of fire, and re-enter the smoke.

A ship's offensive power depended much upon personnel who took no active part in the offensive. Far below, the steersman was housed with compass, wheel and voice tube. The Commander in the engine room overlooked a crew of vast importance—they maintained motive power and preserved the engine fabric. In the crow's nest, the lookout on his swivel chair, was an essential contributor to the whole, with his binoculars and telephone. Below decks, the Torpedo Gunner's Mate made sure that the ship's electricity supply was maintained—without that she was dead. On the bridge was the true control center, for here were the captain, the Navigating Lieutenant, the Torpedo Officer, and the Asdic cabinet. Attendant upon the group was the Yeoman of Signals with his ratings.

All these members of the ship's company, with their fellows, in turn depended upon the Paymaster-Commander, who was responsible for feeding them. In making ready for action, the oil in the ship's cookers was drained, but food could be prepared on a superheated steam pipe. Catering had to be done when opportunity served, to make sure that the men were fortified to meet emergencies. A typical issue would be thick soup, containing tomatoes, corned beef, vegetables, and cornflour, big corned-beef sandwiches, pickles, and cocoa. This was fetched from the galley by the so-called cooks of the various messes—the term really meant waiters. Enamelled iron mess traps were used as food servers.

An ever-present peril at sea, particularly as regards inshore waters, was the mine. It was still an effective weapon in its conventional form, but infinitely more dangerous as employed by the Germans in the 1939 war. Their magnetic mine was used in relatively shallow water. A ship's hull passing over the mine attracted upward a magnetic needle, which closed an electric circuit and fired the 650-pound charge. This menace was neutralized by using five *degaussing* girdles around the ship's hull, to nullify its magnetism. Another device was the *acoustic* mine, actuated by engine sound waves, but it was not fully effective. Engines running at less than eight knots or more than 24 knots did not register on the mine. In the last months of the war the German *pressure mine* or "oyster" was being laid in waters up to 50 feet in depth. It was detonated by the pressure waves set up by the passing of a ship, and it was difficult to sweep.

There is a tendency to stress the U-boat in a way that overshadows the exploits of British submariners, but in fact the British were extremely active. Among the most famous of their underwater seamen was Lieutenant Ben Bryant (now Rear-Admiral Bryant, C.B., D.S.O. (two bars), D.S.C. His extraordinary career, with 40 sinkings, reads like thriller fiction. Admiral Bryant's book *One Man Band* is full of unusual slants on the perilous submarine service. For instance, when under threat of ramming in the Skagerrak, he was unable to go deep quickly, as there is a layer of heavy salt water just below periscope depth. Though the ramming ship struck his submarine, *Sealion*, very heavily, it did not inflict crippling damage. However, the submarine had been flooded so much to get down that, once through the layer, she dropped quickly to danger depth. Frantic action was needed to get her up to a safe level again.

Another dashing leader of seamen was Captain (later Admiral of the Fleet Sir Philip) Vian, whose most famous exploit was the *Altmark* episode. In February 1940 the destroyer *Intrepid* intercepted *Altmark*, a German auxiliary

193

cruiser, off the Norwegian coast. She had aboard the crews of British merchantmen sunk by *Graf Spee* in the South Atlantic; there were 299 seamen all told. *Altmark* took refuge in Josing Fjord, but Captain Vian brought in his destroyer *Cossack* and boarded the prisoner transport in traditional style. As the boarding party swarmed over the deck, rifles in hand, a petty officer shouted down the forehatch: "Any British down there?"

"Yes!" came the bellowed reply.

"Well, the Navy's here!"

In a little over a year—May 1941—Vian commanded the destroyers that took part in the pursuit of *Bismarck*, pride of the new German Navy—35,000 tons and eight 15-inch guns. When the Admiralty received intelligence that *Bismarck* and the heavy cruiser *Prinz Eugen* had left their anchorage in Bergen, Norway, instant action was taken. These powerful vessels were a threat to allied merchantmen. Units of the Royal Navy confronted the two in Denmark Strait, but in the exchange of fire the famous battlecruiser H.M.S. *Hood* was blown up and sunk by *Bismarck*'s shells (May 24).

Though damaged, the latter escaped southward, pursued by aircraft, and she was found again on the 26th. In a fierce action next day, *Bismarck* was pounded by *King George V* and *Rodney*, while being assailed by torpedoes from aircraft and destroyers. Like a trapped lion, the German warship hit out savagely. At last, under the battleships' torrent of shells, every turret on *Bismarck* was silenced. She was ablaze from stem to stern, but still her colors flew. H.M. cruiser *Dorsetshire* was ordered to close in and finish the action with torpedoes, though she hit with three before *Bismarck* turned over and took her dead crew down to a seaman's grave.

14

Peril and Progress

When the United States entered the war in December, 1941, it was to face a proposition that dwarfed to insignificance the German surface navy. Japan's sea strength was superior to the U.S. Navy in every class of ship, and their greatest naval expert, Admiral Yamamotu, was a carrier enthusiast. He had four carriers on the secret list, besides ten in his Pacific fleet as opposed to America's three.

While the Japanese admiral was making mass naval movements early in December, 1941, they were apparently misread in Washington as a threat to the East Indies. Nothing was prepared for defense at Pearl Harbor, in Oahu, the main Hawaiian island. Eight battleships were moored under peacetime conditions, no batteries were on a war footing, and the island's aircraft were drawn up on the landing strip.

During the unexpected Japanese attack of December 7, nearly 200 aircraft, dive bombers and torpedo planes, swept over the anchorage in five waves operating from six carriers. Many American seamen did not realize at first that the attack was not simply an exercise. In every respect the defense was caught napping. Two of the battleships were sunk almost at once, and the rest were so severely damaged that they grounded, keel to bottom, in all but one case. More than 2,400 seamen died in that welter of confusion, and nearly 1,200 suffered wounds. It is true that the Japanese submarine support was ineffectual; they lost their five midget craft and two others, but the operation was brilliantly successful.

An important item for the Japanese was the efficiency of their torpedo service. Constant practice with actual ship targets had brought both weapons and technique to the highest level; in fact, Japanese torpedoes were rated the best in the world. In the U.S. Navy, it was almost the opposite—their undependable torpedoes were a source of frustration. For instance, during an action against Japanese

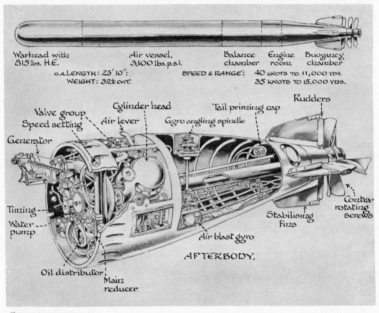

Warhead with 815 lbs. H.E.   Air vessel, 3,100 lbs. p.s.i.   Balance chamber   Engine room   Buoyancy chamber

O.A. LENGTH: 23' 10".   SPEED & RANGE: 40 KNOTS TO 11,000 YDS.
WEIGHT: 32¼ CWT.   35 KNOTS TO 15,000 YDS.

Valve group — Speed setting — Generator — Cylinder head — Air lever — Gyro angling spindle — Tail priming cap — Rudders — Timing — Water pump — Air blast gyro — Stabilising fins — Contra-rotating screws — Oil distributor — Main reducer — AFTERBODY.

21 IN. MARK 9 TORPEDO.

transports off Balikpapan, East Borneo, 48 torpedoes were fired to sink five ships. Even an attempt at magnetic "proximity" exploders, for a near miss, was unsuccessful; in the Southern Hemisphere, the difference in the degree of magnetism affected the torpedo's course. This position was not really amended until 1943.

Meanwhile, the Japanese air-sea onslaught seemed

irresistible. A British Far Eastern force, unwisely taken out into the South China Sea without air cover by Admiral Tom Philips, was hit by more than fifty aircraft. Two battleships, *Repulse* and the new *Prince of Wales*, were sunk. That was the key weapon; the torpedo bomber, backed by a strong naval force, gave Japan command of the Pacific from north to south by early 1942. She had then in her hands the oil and other supplies from the East Indies, and she could establish protection bases there.

An Allied naval group had been set up by that time, comprising American, British, Dutch and Australian warships (ABDA), but the immense Japanese surface power mauled the fleet very severely. It was a combination of ferocious attack, fanatical devotion to the purpose, and superb organization of supply that beat down everything before it. Not until the Allies had begun to strike back with carrier-borne aircraft did the tide turn. Despite the hitting power of the big-gun ships, success lay in the carriers, though they were vulnerable; *Lexington* was so badly hit in the Coral Sea that she caught fire after a violent explosion (May, 1942).

Japanese forces were treated to their own medicine off the Midway Islands in June, 1942—an example of American recovery. Admiral Spruance, in command, had the advantage of the key to the enemy cipher messages, so he despatched a carrier-borne force in an effort to hit the Japanese aircraft before they left their carriers. Though the American attack became disorganized through separation, and most of the torpedo craft were lost through attacking first, the dive bombers gave a tremendous follow-up. No Japanese torpedoplane had left the carriers, owing to the American attack, and their fighters were too low after dealing with the torpedo strike. This permitted 1,000-pound bombs to land on the Japanese carriers, with shattering effect. Three were blown up and fired at once, and a fourth was sunk soon afterward. This was a severe blow, both physically and morally, as defeat was intolerable to the Japanese. They had the satisfaction of shattering a vital convoy two months later, when U.S. Marines were being transported for the first offensive on the Solomon Islands. In a rapid action, the Japanese heavy cruisers sank four of the convoy cruisers and damaged three other warships very badly.

However, the naval effort of Japan was undermined by the shooting down of their great organizer, Admiral Yamamotu, over the Solomons in June, 1943. This loss, and the build-up of material and technique in the U.S. Navy, began to bear hard on the conquerors of the Pacific. By early 1944, terrific blows were being struck against Japanese forces. One most decisive campaign began in February. In the Marshall Islands, U.S. Navy aircraft flew 30 missions in succession, supported by stupendous naval shellfire.

Off the New Guinea coast, at Saipan Island, Admiral Toyoda expected reinforcements for his fleet of nine carriers and five battleships, when he engaged a U.S. force of fifteen carriers and nine battleships. In fact, the Japanese base had been too mangled to supply aircraft, and a crushing defeat awaited Toyoda. He lost 400 aircraft, and the subsequent pursuit and strike completed a near-annihilation. This final blow was delivered by U.S. Navy flyers who knew that their chances of return were doubtful. Nevertheless, the task was gallantly carried out, though a number of aircrew were lost through emergency landing.

During the closing months of that year, the battle for the Pacific waters was fought out around the Philippine Islands, where the Japanese forces were grouped for a major attack. Here the new and the traditional sea weapons, carrier-borne bomber and ponderous battleship, met in tremendous conflict. Japan had two immense warships, *Yamato* and *Musashi*, mounting 18-inch guns, but the latter was sunk by air attack. After a to-and-fro struggle, with a confused

198

ending, the Japanese Navy had lost three battleships, four carriers, seven heavy and four light cruisers, and nine destroyers. It never appeared in action again as a navy.

A desperate new venture was seen in that engagement—the first use of the *kamikaze*, the suicide aircraft loaded as a piloted bomb. *St. Lo*, a U.S. Navy carrier, was blown up by one of these, and two other carriers were hit. This weapon was increasingly employed, with a good deal of success. In fact, when the Americans were closing in, with attacks on Kyushu, the southern island of Japan itself, all Japanese air strikes were decreed as *kamikaze*, six at a time. Their air

POCKET BATTLESHIP 'ADMIRAL GRAF SPEE'.

losses became stupendous, running into thousands on Okinawa alone.

This gigantic struggle showed that the fighting seaman in war had to take to the air for survival, and that the day of the great warship, the "battle wagon," was done. One really tremendous last operation was afforded the latter—fire support for the Allied invasion of Normandy on June 6, 1944. There was seen for the last time a mighty line of capital ships—*Ramillies, Nelson*, and their massive companions, hurling their one-ton shells to roar overhead like express trains and thunder doom upon the defenders' works. Fiery support was given by the gallant destroyers and U.S.

199

Navy rocket ships; they ran almost on to the beach, so close inshore was their fire delivered. One salvo from a rocket ship equalled the gunfire of 200 destroyers.

Under cover of that torrent of bursting steel, in to the beach crept the clumsy assault craft, manned by Merchant Navy seamen. Those sons of Britain, who had for years risked their lives to bring in life-giving supplies to the homeland, had the proud task of carrying into action the forces of liberation.

While the Western Europeans and their American brothers were waging desperate battle in their own theaters of war, Russia was striving to thrust the German invader from her lands. In the war at sea, the Russians had been largely on the defensive, which was aided by their big submarine build-up in 1940. Surface craft lagged as regards building rate—a light carrier took nearly three years to complete.

At that time, the navy was a more significant part of Soviet military power than it had ever been. Since 1935, when the new naval ensign was first worn—white, with a red five-point star, hammer and sickle—a great drive had been made to equate it with the massive land forces. On July 28, 1939, Red Navy Day was observed for the first time, and the solemn oath of the newly enrolled seaman was impressive:

"I, a citizen of the Union of Socialist Soviet Republics, entering the ranks of the Workers' and Peasants' Red Navy, do take oath and swear to be an honorable, brave, disciplined, and watchful fighter, to keep strictly all naval secrets, to fulfil obediently all naval regulations, and the orders of commanders, commissars, and chiefs.

"I swear to apply myself conscientiously to acquiring knowledge of naval affairs, to guard unsleepingly the naval and national possessions, to remain devoted to my last breath to my people, to my Soviet Fatherland, and to the Workers' and Peasants' Government.

"I shall ever be ready at the command of the Workers' and

Peasants' Government to go forward for the defense of my Fatherland, the Union of Socialist Soviet Republics, and as a fighter of the Workers' and Peasants' Red Navy, I swear to defend her with courage, with skill, with dignity and with honor, sparing neither my blood nor my life to achieve victory over the enemy.

"If of malice I betray this my solemn oath, then let me be visited with the strict punishment of Soviet law, general hatred, and the contempt of all working people."

He then donned the black ribboned cap and the blue and white barrel-striped jersey, to begin the new extended period

H.M.S. EXETER.

of service (five years) which Stalin decreed in 1939. A great part of the Red Navy's work was to keep open the vital northern route for British merchant ships carrying war materials to aid Russia's struggle after the German invasion of June, 1941. Arctic convoy duty, shared with the Royal Navy, was the most desperate undertaking for seamen in both warship and freightship. U-boats sinking the laboring vessels condemned the crews to death in those ice-bound waters. Briton and Russian battled side by side against the wolf of the sea. An interesting survival of the old link between the two was the loan of H.M.S. *Royal Sovereign* to the Red Navy

201

G*

in 1944. There she was renamed *Archangelsk*, and she remained on strength until her return in 1949.

Sea service abounds in the unsung heroes, those who do not figure in combat, but whose service is vital. There was an epic occasion after the surrender of the Belgian army in May, 1940. With remarkable forethought, the British Government

PEARL HARBOUR
Direct hit on magazine of destroyer 'Shaw.'

had already made a register of all the small, privately owned seaworthy vessels in the Kingdom. When the news came that the British Expeditionary Force, exposed by the Belgian defection, had been pressed back to Dunkirk, a unique rescue fleet crossed the Channel. About four hundred and fifty vessels composed the fleet, and more than half of them were the "little ships" of amateur seamen. Every imaginable type

202

was there; the fishing boat, the cabin cruiser, the auxiliary sailing boat converged on the perilous beach regardless of gunfire and swooping aircraft. Three hundred thousand men were brought home in that motley fleet, the most extraordinary operation in the annals of the sea.

On the other side of the world, another unheard-of organization was created by the Pearl Harbor disaster. This was the Seabees group, formed of Naval Construction Battalions under the control of the U.S. Navy's Civil Engineer Corps. Seabees specialized in construction—and reconstruction—of naval bases for war. There were 200,000 of these men, trained as Marines, jeering at their own peculiar status in doing civilian work for Service pay. In fact, the combatant units owed much to the cheerful ingenuity of the Seabees, and it was obvious that, when the base was under attack, a bullet made no distinction between the two.

While the unorthodox is being considered, there were two forms of attack upon ships in anchorage that called for picked seamen of the hardiest. One was the manned torpedo, an Italian device first employed in the Mediterranean in 1917. By means of a saddle and controls, the operator could steer until he was true upon his target, when he would slip off and swim clear. This idea was much elaborated by the Italian navy in the 1939 war. Their S.L.C. torpedo was battery-driven, with windshield, compass and depth gauge. Trim was maintained by a power pump that adjusted the water ballast between forward and after tanks. S.L.C. was manned by an officer, and a seaman, with oxygen helmets to permit a dive at need.

By 1943, both Britain and Germany were making use of the manned torpedo. *Neger*, the German type, towed a standard torpedo, so that two weapons hit in succession. It was a perilous position for the riders at best, but with a menace behind them as well the mission needed an iron nerve. Mortality was high among these intrepid seamen, on

203

both sides. When the British planned to use manned torpedoes against German warships lying in the Norwegian fjords, the crews had to undergo further hardening. Northern waters at 7°C were a different proposition from the Mediterranean, so training was done in the ice-cold lochs of Scotland.

TORPEDOMEN AND FROGMEN.

Even more desperate was the undertaking of the *frogman*, with protective suit and breathing gear. He had flexible froglike flippers on his feet, and his task was to swim under anchored ships and stick on *limpet bombs*.

One of the most valuable devices of the war was radar observation for shipping and aircraft, as regards both protection and attack. This was used in locating an object by

204

radio waves without co-operation by the object itself. Radar (Radio Angle, Direction, and Range) was developed for military use by a team of British scientists led by (Sir) Robert Watson-Watt, in 1935. For ship navigation it was invaluable, recording on its screen the shape of nearby objects in fog or darkness, such as a ship or a coastline. These features were flooded with radio waves, and reflected waves were recorded on a television-type screen, showing the shape of the objects. Apart from its military value radar was invaluable to navigators; by using radar and getting a radio fix from the

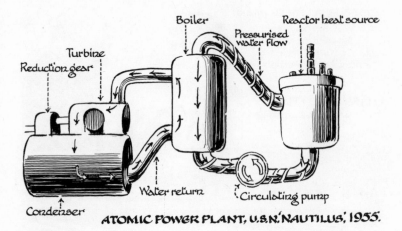

ATOMIC POWER PLANT, U.S.N. 'NAUTILUS', 1955.

shore station, much of the drudgery was taken out of navigation.

Soon after the war, when America concentrated on the application of atomic power, the target became an atomic submarine. In January, 1955, the first vessel of that kind, named *Nautilus*, was sent out on trials from Groton, Connecticut. She measured 300 feet by 28 feet, displacing 2,980 tons submerged, and her original cost was £10,357,000, two-thirds of that figure being the cost of the atomic plant. In the latter, atoms were split in a reactor, generating terrific heat. A force pump circulated pressurized water through the reactor. Being under pressure, the water did not become steam, but it acted as a "heat exchanger," carrying the atomic heat to the boiler. From the boiler, superheated steam passed to the turbines, thence to the condenser, and into the boiler again as water. It is fairly certain that this vessel was capable of more than thirty knots under water, and she cruised 60,000 miles on her original charge—eight pounds of enriched uranium.

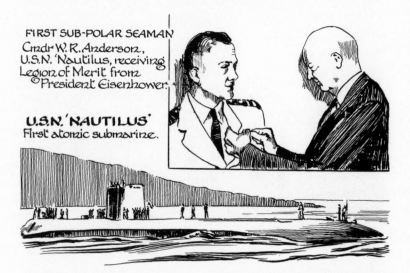

FIRST SUB-POLAR SEAMAN
Cmdr W. R. Anderson,
U.S.N. 'Nautilus, receiving
Legion of Merit from
President Eisenhower.

U.S.N. 'NAUTILUS'
First atomic submarine.

Nautilus was manned by 108 officers and seamen, the latter being messed in groups of 12. There was more room aboard than a submarine usually provided, and there was even a jukebox for light entertainment. With such a vessel the submarine's function was materially changed. No longer was it a submersible surface vessel, but one designed to operate below and to remain there for long periods. This was possible through the manufacture of "potted air" aboard.

On her way to Britain, in October, 1957, *Nautilus* travelled

5,007 miles under water, at an average of 15 knots, and in early August, 1958, she made an epic voyage under the North Pole. This began at Port Barrow, Northern Alaska; the submarine passed under pack ice to come up off Spitzbergen, Norway, 96 hours later. While the captain, Commander Anderson, was under the actual Pole, he found a curious

Submarine ace, 1942.
COMMANDER BEN BRYANT, R.N.

navigational position. There was no direction other than south, so the gyrocompass could not function. In its place an inertial system was used, like the old-time seaman's dead reckoning. It was a stable platform that kept its level and pointer direction no matter how the ship moved. Anderson reported nearly 13,500 feet of water at the Pole, and an icecap ten to fifteen feet thick.

At that time there was much speculation about the use of the Polar route for commercial traffic, as it cut 5,000 miles off west-to-east sea routes, but nothing more transpired. America's second nuclear submarine, *Sea Wolf*, 3,260 tons, was launched in 1955. She created an absolute underwater record, in 1958, by remaining below for 60 days. As *Sea Wolf* was out of contact with the earth's atmosphere, it was rightly judged that U977's *schnorkel*-assisted dive of 66 days in 1945 was outclassed. Observers remarked, though, that *Sea Wolf*'s crew looked pale and languid, and that they eagerly gulped the fresh air when they came on deck after the prolonged dive.

Medical science was deeply involved in the study of the physical effects regarding long-term diving. In December 1958, a group of U.S. Navy doctors published a report of one detrimental effect—the seamen's teeth deteriorated at twice the normal rate. Radiation was prevented by heavily screening the ship's reactors, so some other cause had to be sought, noise, excessive carbon in the atmosphere, or absence of a day-and-night change when submerged. No positive reason for the condition has been found.

In March, 1959, the third U.S. Navy craft of the type, *Skate*, made her second voyage under the Pole—her first had been a few days after *Nautilus*. In *Skate*'s survey of ice and water, between ten and seventy feet of ice were recorded, with water two miles deep. Once the vessel cut through several inches of ice to surface, and Commander James Calvert, her captain, remarked on the *polynas* (lakes in the ice) big enough for *Skate* to cruise upon.

While that Arctic adventure was going on, *Skipjack* went on trial, the first fourdecker submarine, with really spacious crews' quarters for the seamen in the complement of over a hundred. Every bunk was fitted with a reading lamp and a switch to control ventilation. A daily film show was provided, and the library contained 600 books. This was unheard-of comfort, even for American ships, and it was likely to be increased by crew reduction. A device called a *subic controls,* was put forward in 1959, whereby a dozen men with a push-button system could work and fight the submarine with ease. However, this was still only in the preparatory stage ten years later.

When the underwater seaman was thus provided with a long-term diving ship, his next acquisition was a missile to be projected into the atmosphere. After many experiments, *George Washington*, 5,400 tons, was launched in June, 1959, as the U.S. Navy's first missile submarine. She carried 16 solid-fuel *Polaris* nuclear missiles, 30 feet by 5 feet, which were fired by compressed air to range 1,500 miles. Firing was done under the guidance of the superaccurate navigation method used in the Polar voyages—S.I.N.S., (Ship Inertia Navigation System). *George Washington* fired the first underwater *Polaris* shot in July, 1960; it registered on target at 1,100 miles (Cape Canaveral, Florida (now Cape Kennedy) to a point north of Puerto Rico).

Despite the remarkable technical advances in submarines of the 1960 decade, they were not completely safe, so losses still occurred. This led to acute concentration on escape from sunken craft, either by the bell method or by "free escape." One form of the latter was adopted by the Royal Navy in 1957. An inflatable suit was worn, and the escapee filled his mouth with a mixture of 60-40 nitrogen and oxygen. He rose rapidly to the surface as the air was expelled from his open mouth, and on breaking surface his suit floated.

Escape by the Rescue Bell entailed having the conning tower of the submarine previously fitted with special equipment. Its main hatch carried a large central eye to take the hook of a downhaul cable which drew the bell down into position. There were seating plates on each side of the conning tower, on which the bell settled. Rubber gaskets around the base formed a seal, and holding-down bolts were secured to eyes on the seatings. Two compartments made up the interior, the lower one being open to the sea. When the bell was sealed in position, this lower compartment was blown clear of water. An exit hatch in the main conning tower hatch was then opened, and a group of seamen could scramble up into the lower compartment. A hatch suspended

First atomic carrier
85,000 tons
5-acre flight deck

U.S. AIRCRAFT-CARRIER 'ENTERPRISE', 1961.

from centrally placed tackle was lowered to give access to the upper section. When the hatch was replaced, and the conning tower secured, the bell was hoisted clear of the submarine to carry the group of survivors to the surface.

This escape system did not prove altogether satisfactory, so the U.S. Navy adopted a free escape method for all but the largest craft. A hood apparatus, providing trapped air, was designed by Lieutenant Steinke, U.S.N. He and Commander Mazzone made a record escape at 361 feet, from the U.S. submarine *Balao*, in 1961. British authorities introduced a similar hood in 1962, and in late 1968 a further development was made by a former Royal Navy officer and a civilian. Lieutenant-Commander Laurence Hamlyn and Mr. Kenneth Tayler designed a cotton fabric hood, with a plastic face piece, and covering head and shoulders. In operation, the wearer went into a one-man escape cylinder inside the submarine; the cylinder had an outside cap like a torpedo tube. As soon as it had been flooded, and the cap opened, the escapee floated up by means of the air trapped in the hood.

Britain's first nuclear submarine, *Dreadnought*, with an American power plant, was launched at the Vickers-Armstrongs yard, Barrow-in-Furness, by Her Majesty Queen Elizabeth II. It was fitting that the launching took place on Trafalgar Day, October 21, 1960. *Dreadnought* was 266 feet by 32 feet by 3,500 tons, and her hull was of the "teardrop" design that permits high underwater speed. *Valiant*, of 1963, was the first all-British nuclear submarine.

This accent on undersea craft reflected the naval policy of the principal navies of the world; in fact, Russia was reported as having the largest fleet in this respect. A pattern of submarines, light surface craft, and aircraft carriers became general among western nations, though the large carriers remained vulnerable in air attack.

Submarine detection was greatly advanced in 1960, with the Canadian development of a Variable Depth Asdic Set ("The Assassin"). It was claimed that the device could pinpoint a submarine at a range of 75 miles, where previous detector gear could not exceed three miles. A further step by Aga, the Swedish cooker company, produced in 1965 a closed-circuit television apparatus that recorded the change of temperature created by the presence of a nuclear submarine in a stretch of water. Positive antisubmarine action

211

was provided by a new torpedo developed at Portland by the Admiralty. Homing torpedoes of various types still existed, and the German navy of 1939—45 had used an electric weapon. This new type of 1968 was a wireguided electric torpedo, with a wide-angle sonar in the nose, and a proximity fuse.

THE ONLY SERVING BATTLESHIP.
U.S.N. 'New Jersey' in action off Viet-Nam, 1968.

Britain's last venture into big battleships was H.M.S. *Vanguard*, launched in 1944. This great vessel, of 42,000 tons, cost £12,000,000, and was never in action. She was placed "in reserve" in 1956, and scrapped three years later. There is only one operational battleship in the world at the time of writing—the U.S.N. *New Jersey*, 56,000 tons. She was brought out of "mothballs" in the late summer of

1968 to add her 16-inch shells to the torrent of fire poured upon Vietcong positions. Curiously, the Royal Navy's *first* armored ship still survives. H.M.S. *Warrior* forms part of an oil jetty at Pembroke Docks, in Wales. During 1968 a move began to preserve and restore the old ironclad.

Survivals present strange problems. In September, 1967, a

RUSSIAN SEAMEN, 1969: CRUISER 'OCTOBER REVOLUTION.'

diver off Start Point, in Devonshire, found the 1918 submarine monitor M1, which sank with all hands in 1925. She was an experimental craft, mounting a 12-inch gun. A salvage expert, Captain Silas Oates, proposed to raise M1 by piping in compressed air, but the Ministry of Defence (Navy) forbade this. "She is the tomb of sixty-nine brave men, and to the Royal Navy she is sacrosanct."

213

In sea-girt Britain, the followers of the sea have always a special brotherhood, in spite of their wide variety. Around the British coasts, there are still numbers of old seamen, with deep indelible tan, in the thick blue jersey that is still called a "slop," after the old-time shipboard issue. Yet the present-day Royal Navy rating rarely shows that weather-beaten tan, for a great proportion of the crew serve below decks, or are otherwise enclosed. Traditional hardihood is still to be found, however, among those seamen who face the elements in drifter and trawler, to toss and plunge in home waters or in the icy seas of the north. These intrepid fishermen have the leathery toughness of their forbears, the seamen of the days in sail.

During a century of progress, the seaman technician loomed larger with the passing years, until at the present day he is the service itself. Such complicated guidance, control, and weapon systems are to be manned that every rating has a responsible position. Promotion to petty officer almost always calls for high-level specialist qualifications, while achievement of the two seaman grades needs in most cases a speciality—always, in fact, for Leading Seaman. Good conduct badges on the left arm rarely serve alone for promotion to Able Seaman; it is only certain if the right arm bears a specialist badge.

This change in the seaman's environment was the official reason for stopping the traditional rum issue, as from July 31st, 1970. Throughout the world, on that day, the Royal Navy personnel mourned the passing of an important feature of their economy. It had provided for payment of small debts, barter, the honouring of guests, and settlement of wagers for more than 300 years. During much of that time senior ratings had drawn neat spirit, 95% proof, while juniors received grog.

As compensation for the blow, ratings were allowed to buy three 1s 1d cans of canteen beer per day instead of two. They could afford this, as their pay had increased. Under the pay scales of 1968, the able seaman drew £11 14s. 6d a week, and a leading seaman of 23 was paid £14 17s. 6d. These rates were allied with kit issue, varied and palatable meals, and comfortable quarters. It was a far cry from 24s. a month, purser's clothing, hardtack, and 16 inches of hammock room per man.

Still the sea is there, with its compelling urge. Whatever form of propulsion may be used on it, the fascination remains to draw on the adventurous. Within recent years, a number of lone voyages have created controversy. On the one side, the ancient call, and the challenge of skill pitted against the power of wind and sea; on the other, the practical view that, if the solitary voyager is lost, thousands of pounds are poured out in the search for him. It may be that these ventures, even if foolhardy, are a form of rebellion against the mechanical age, a defiant gesture by the seaman.

Index

INDEX

INDEX

Typesetting by Print Origination Liverpool L20 6NS

Printed in Great Britain by
Page Bros (Norwich) Ltd.,
London and Norwich